T0284087

A HAUNTED HISTORY OF GRAND RAPIDS

JULIE RATHSACK

Haunted America

Published by Haunted America
A Division of The History Press
Charleston, SC
www.historypress.com

Copyright © 2024 by Julie Rathsack
All rights reserved

First published 2024

Manufactured in the United States

ISBN 9781467157278

Library of Congress Control Number: 2024936790

Notice: The information in this book is true and complete to the best of our knowledge. It is offered without guarantee on the part of the author or The History Press. The author and The History Press disclaim all liability in connection with the use of this book.

All rights reserved. No part of this book may be reproduced or transmitted in any form whatsoever without prior written permission from the publisher except in the case of brief quotations embodied in critical articles and reviews.

This book is dedicated to my grandma and grandpa Lucille and Thaddeus Wojtowicz. My childhood is filled with countless cherished memories, all thanks to the two of you and the beautiful family you created. You will forever hold a special place in our hearts!

CONTENTS

ACKNOWLEDGEMENTS

This book would have been impossible without the following people (in no particular order):

FAMILY: My remarkable husband, David Rathsack, who continues to remind me that I can accomplish anything I put my mind to. My boys, David Julian and Samuel Joseph: I am so proud of both of you! My parents, Gene and Vicki Krzeminski. You've both been there for me every step of the way, and I am who I am because of you. (Thanks a lot!)

FRIENDS: Brad Donaldson, my fabulous photographer and even better friend. I already miss our Sunday morning picture runs! Roger Scholz, my talented buddy (and boo) at Wicked Illustration. Without you asking me how much I got done on my book every time I saw you, it would still be unfinished on my laptop. Bob Webster, for making every investigation amusing, chaps and all. Jeff Sytsma, my historian friend and partner in crime. I did my book, now do yours! Nicole and Rob DuShane: it took eight years, but I got it done! It's crazy what being locked in a closet can lead to. Jim Winslow, my go-to when I need a quick answer about where something used to be located in Grand Rapids. Connor Jobbins, my incredible godson, for coming on my tours and hanging out with me. You are a cool guy, and we need to do more together! My future golden girls: Jennifer Falicki, Kelly Glover, Heather Burke and Amy Jo Parent. Thank you for being a friend.

OTHER SOURCES: Carol Dodge, for sharing your vast knowledge of the Sweets and their beautiful home. Alex Forist and Andrea Melvin, curators at the Grand Rapids Public Museum, for always responding to the crazy ghost lady's emails. Gina Geglio, your passion for our city's history is palpable, and you inspire me to do more. Todd Almassian, for trusting me with your prized folder and inviting me into your home. Mary T. Dersch, curator at the East Grand Rapids History Room. Pam VanderPloeg from Grand Rapids Downtown Buildings. Tony Wright, the city archives officer for the City of Grand Rapids. The descendants of characters in our stories: Kathie Dillard Schwend, Sarah Boye and George Hibben. And finally, Father Dennis Morrow, who has since passed on. One of the last times we discussed history, you wrote to me, "We all have a limited amount of time on Earth, but I do my best to leave behind a little more knowledge gathered and better organized than the way I found it!" This is my goal as well. Consider your mission accomplished. Thank you for all your hard work and dedication in collecting our city's history. I'm sure you are up there telling Jesus all about it.

PREFACE

One of my favorite memories from when I was a kid is of sitting in the unfinished basement of my childhood home in the dark. With only the faint light seeping in from the four small windows that lined the exterior walls, dark shadows fell everywhere. A big, creepy furnace stood in the middle of the room, blocking out any light that dared filter through. I sat in a circle with my brother Joe and my sisters Heather and Jennifer, all of us so silent we could hear each other breathe. Joe would lean in and, in his creepiest Vincent Price–like voice, begin to tell the story of the ghost that lived in the tiny room in the far back area of our cellar.

Her name was Lucy. She and her husband, John, lived in our home before our dad purchased it. Lucy was known about town for her beauty. She had striking eyes with full eyelashes and lovely long red hair that she would spend hours brushing. The only unattractive thing about her was that she knew how appealing others found her and would use it to her advantage. Despite being married, she would flirt with other men, who, in turn, would shower her with gifts.

John, who once considered himself the luckiest man in the world, began to realize his wife was unfaithful. One day, he walked into the house after a hard day's work and found Lucy opening a package from yet another unidentified man. Her eyes glazed over as she smiled and held a shiny sterling silver hairbrush up to the light. It was all too much for John. He lunged forward, wrapped his hands around her neck and choked her until she lost consciousness. Reaching over, he grabbed a pair of sewing scissors that were lying on a chest nearby and cut off her precious flowing red hair—the ultimate humiliation.

He dragged Lucy's lifeless body to the basement, determined to dismember and bury her. As he raised the axe above his head and began to bring it down toward her neck, Lucy opened her eyes in horror. Blood spattered everywhere as the blow connected. Her head rolled across the room. Unfazed, John continued cutting her body up, tossing each body part into a hole in the cellar. He then covered her with cold, damp earth and spent hours cleaning up. It wasn't until he had finished making the floor look completely undisturbed that he remembered her head. As he picked it up, he began to realize what he had done. He wailed as he lifted her head close to him and kissed the cold lips of his former sweetheart. Filled with grief and unable to live with himself, John went down to the Grand River and threw himself off the Sixth Street Bridge. He drowned. Lucy's head was never found.

At that exact point in the story, our brother Mike would roll a woman's mannequin head down the basement steps. It would hit the wall at the bottom with a thud and come to a standstill, vacant eyes staring blankly at nothing. We would all scream and go running up the stairs.

This silly prank played itself out over and over. I loved hearing the same cheesy story, capped off with a fright. I was hooked. Even as I got older and found out it was completely made up, I continued to appreciate it for what it was—a good creepy story. From that moment on, I did everything I could to lay my hands on books filled with ghost stories. I'm not sure what happened to Lucy the mannequin head, but she and my siblings had set me on the path of loving a spooky tale.

To top it off, when I was about eight years old, I began to experience unexplainable activity around my home. (No, Lucy's head had nothing to do with it.) I'd see shadow figures walk through the room and witness objects move by themselves. Unexplained voices were heard on a regular basis—primarily by my mother and me, as well as an occasional friend who would dare spend the night. I found myself able to sense when something was about to happen. The air would change, and a heaviness would overcome me. Seconds later, an unexplained event would occur. I jokingly called it my "ghosty sense."

I discovered the book *Haunted Houses of Grand Rapids* by the late Don W. Farrant in the late 1980s. It was comforting to find that other people in Grand Rapids were dealing with hauntings as well. When the book was revised by Gary Eberle and John Layman in 1994, I found myself playing

Lucy's mannequin head at the bottom of the steps. *Roger Scholz.*

detective. It became my mission to try and find out where all the homes in the book were located. (Out of all the chapters, only two of the locations remain a mystery to me.) Anytime I drove by the homes, I'd point them out to my family and friends and relate the tales of their dark past. I even

My childhood home. *Brad Donaldson.*

convinced my mom to pretend to be interested in purchasing the old Phillips Mansion on Prospect Avenue when it was up for sale in June 1994 so I could get inside. While she kept the realtor busy, I snooped through the place, taking endless pictures and looking in every nook and cranny. (For more on the Phillips Mansion, see chapter 5 in *Ghosts of Grand Rapids.*) It became my passion to collect ghost stories from my city.

At nineteen, I began to work part-time at a company located on the fourteenth floor of the McKay Tower. It worked out great, as it was situated in the middle of downtown Grand Rapids, blocks away from the college I attended. Between work and classes, I would wander about the city, taking in all the unique buildings and learning about their history. I became known about town as Ghosty Girl. I never thought twice about walking into a place and saying, "This building is old. Have you ever experienced anything paranormal here?" No matter the response, I documented it in a notebook, as I knew that one day, I would author my own book on our great city's ghosts.

I joined the West Michigan Ghost Hunters Society (WMGHS) in 2001 and, over the years, have become very close with the other members: Nicole Du Shane (Bray), Brad Donaldson, Bob Weber and Roger Scholz. I collaborated on my debut book, *Ghosts of Grand Rapids*, alongside Nicole Du Shane (Bray) and Robert Du Shane, who had previously coauthored other books. They also led successful ghost tours in Kalamazoo with their company Paranormal Michigan (www.ParanormalMichigan.com). In 2015, we launched the original Ghosts of Grand Rapids Outdoor Walking Tour. Our inaugural tour attracted just seven attendees, but by the end of the season, demand had skyrocketed. We were soon scheduling several tours a week, and each one sold out. To maintain a manageable group size, we capped ticket sales at fifty. While other tour groups have come and gone, ours consistently receives rave reviews. Not only do we possess extensive knowledge of the city's eerie history, but we can also substantiate it with real facts. Unlike some other tours that attribute every flickering light to the paranormal, we provide honest insights. As a seasoned ghost hunter with thirty years of experience, I'll tell you the unvarnished truth. Over time, Nicole and Rob took charge of the original west route, while I designed a new east route. My trusty notebooks proved invaluable, as I had collected personal stories from people all over the downtown area spanning three decades. Whenever I found a newspaper article and could tie it to a ghostly sighting or a paranormal experience I had previously documented, it was like solving a puzzle. I hope you appreciate the culmination of my efforts and enjoy reading the following stories as much as I enjoyed putting them together.

CHAPTER 1
THE MISSING MONEY

LOCATION: CORNER OF FOUNTAIN STREET AND IONIA AVENUE

A lfred Morse Webster was a good man, honest and hardworking. He was born in Richland, Michigan, and became a schoolteacher in 1868 at the age of nineteen. After holding the job of superintendent of the Monroe school system, he went on to graduate from the Chicago Homeopathic College and became a physician and surgeon with Ruffe and Webster. His one goal in life was to help others. One person who knew him said, "Alfred believed that whatever was worth doing was worth doing well. He had the constant aim of doing good." He was also active as a Mason and a member of Woodmen of the World.

While he had a successful career, Alfred was not as fortunate in his personal life. At twenty-one, he married Caroline Donaldson, also a schoolteacher, and together they had a little boy they named Eugene. Sadly, when Eugene was only three, his mom passed away from peritonitis. A year later, Alfred married nineteen-year-old Hattie Hale, and they had two daughters, Ida and Ruey. Unfortunately, his second wife died just ten years later, once again leaving Alfred alone with his children. He successfully raised them into thriving, successful adults, and they settled in Grand Rapids, where Alfred worked as the general secretary for the New Era Association Insurance Company. He also helped several family members get jobs at the firm, including his son-in-law Charles McGuire, who was married to his oldest daughter, Ida. At fifty-eight years old, Alfred married his third wife, Hattie Dubbs. Hattie was eighteen at the time of the wedding, three years younger than Alfred's youngest child, Ruey.

Right: Alfred Morse Webster. *Courtesy of Kathie Dillard Schwend.*

Below: 82 Ionia Avenue, former site of the New Era Association Insurance Company. *Brad Donaldson.*

It was a brisk day on September 30, 1909. As the leaves blew around in circles at his feet, insurance examiner Engelhart walked toward the three-story building that sat on the southeast corner of Fountain Street and Ionia Avenue. It was Thursday, and he was on his way to interview Alfred. The night before, Engelhart had found a discrepancy in the company's bank account in the amount of $14,594 (the equivalent of approximately $501,000 in 2024). He was eager to figure out where the money went.

On arriving, Engelhart found the doors closed and locked. He sat outside until Charles McGuire, Alfred's son-in-law and coworker, showed up and let him in. Together, they walked upstairs to the second floor, where the company's offices were located. McGuire excused himself and went to get Alfred from his office.

When Charles opened the door, he found his father-in-law lying on the couch in the corner, covered in blood. He ran over, but it was too late. It seemed obvious from the bullet hole in Alfred's chest and the revolver by his side that his wound was self-inflicted. The doctor had carefully taken off his coat and vest, unbuttoned his shirt and shot himself clear through the heart.

When his family and friends began to think back over the previous days, it became apparent that something had been off with Alfred. Engelhart and Alfred had spent Tuesday together at the office, balancing the books. Alfred, a man well known for his cheerful demeanor, showed no signs that anything was wrong as they worked. On Wednesday, however, Alfred called in sick, claiming that his doctor had confined him to the house. He and Engelhart spoke by phone later in the day, and Alfred said he would be in the office the following morning. He gave no clue that Engelhart would find him dead. Next to his lifeless body was a suicide note that stated he had turned over all funds in his charge, except those that he fairly earned.

> *I have fought a losing fight. I tried to allow no smirch on my good name, but I could not have a home while I was doing so. I "fought graft in higher places" and all the powers and principalities in the world were against me. I have earned all I ever got from the New Era, and more. I have given honest service, but if there is anything yet due, I pay it now with all my heart.*

As the investigation into his death went on, it became evident that Dr. Webster knew he was going to be called to answer for the missing funds. Rumors began to circulate that the reason he was ill on Wednesday was that he attempted suicide on Tuesday night by taking morphine at his home, but it didn't kill him. Everyone who knew Alfred struggled to accept that he would have done any of this.

Kathie Dillard Schwend is Alfred's great-granddaughter (Eugene was her grandfather). She shared that soon after Alfred's demise, the entire family moved to Houston, Texas. When she asked about her great-grandfather's death, her family told her that Alfred had found out he had a brain tumor, and that is why he shot himself. Since no other evidence has ever shown up to support this claim, she suspects it is her family's way of justifying his suicide without tarnishing his good name.

Alfred was not one to squander money or act recklessly. Where the funds disappeared to was never proven, but some found it quite coincidental that Dr. Webster was in the process of constructing a new bungalow on the west end of Reeds Lake, a home that was supposed to cost around $15,000. Construction was never completed while the house was in the hands of the Webster family. Alfred's young wife signed over the house, which sat on seventeen acres of forest land, to the New Era Association immediately after Alfred's death.

Charles McGuire, the son-in-law who found Alfred's body, quickly stepped into Alfred's role at the company as the general secretary—beneficial to him,

The bungalow Alfred Morse Webster built on Reed's Lake. *Courtesy of the East Grand Rapids History Room.*

but not necessarily suspicious. What does seem sketchy is that Charles later divorced Alfred's daughter Ida and went on to marry Alfred's widow, Hattie. Could the two have had a hidden relationship prior? Taking it a step further, could Alfred have been set up or even murdered? All have passed on now and remain innocent until proven otherwise.

As for the home, the company sold it in 1910 to a man from Milwaukee named Hans Mills. His original plan was to live there and raise frogs to sell to local restaurants, as frog legs were all the rage at the time. He eventually used it as a boardinghouse for several years before selling it to Eli Epstein, who worked at a local haberdashery. After Epstein's death in 1970, the home fell into disrepair and was demolished in 1973.

THE HAUNTING

The only thing that remains of the home are the stone columns that once stood at the opening of the driveway. They continue to stand proudly in front of what is now the entrance to Waterfront Park on Lakeside Drive. There are many reports of hauntings in the area but none that are necessarily tied to this property. Countless drownings and accidents have occurred around Reeds Lake, so it would be difficult to prove that any paranormal activity stems from Webster's original homestead.

On the other hand, it is believed that the location where Alfred took his life is still haunted by the past. The office building was originally a three-floor structure built in 1901, with the fourth floor being added in 1932. Many different businesses have come and gone throughout the years. It is currently owned by Kent County and is home to the Circuit Court Probation Office. In 2016, Kendall College of Art and Design had hopes of acquiring the property and using it for student housing. Alas, the building would not allow for the kind of renovations needed, causing the deal to fall through. The county continues to receive bids on the desirable property but has yet to part with the building.

I spoke with a woman named Rosa who was a member of the crew that cleaned the building at night, usually after everyone else had gone home. She has worked at many different locations throughout downtown Grand Rapids but freely admits that the building at 82 Ionia is the only one she dreads going into.

The original stone columns from the bungalow's driveway. *Brad Donaldson.*

One night several years back, Rosa started to clean the third floor with one other person from her crew. It was around nine o'clock, and most lights in the building were off. Realizing they had forgotten the broom on the previous floor, she entered the elevator and pushed the down button. As the elevator came to rest on the second floor and the doors opened, the main light in the hallway began to flicker. Rosa assumed it was a bad bulb and exited the elevator. As she walked down the hall toward the last office they had been in, she began to feel as if she were being watched. She turned around several times but saw no one.

As she entered the corner office, the light automatically turned on. Nervously, she began to walk toward the broom, which was propped up against the wall. She grabbed the handle, turned around and came face-to-face with a well-dressed older gentleman standing directly in front of her. She screamed and dropped the broom. "I'm sorry! You startled me!" she apologized, assuming it to be an employee who was still in the building. As she bent over to pick up the broom, she noticed his clothing seemed a bit odd—as if his business attire had been purchased from a vintage store. Wanting to get out of his way, she smiled and exited the room. As she turned to tell him to have a good night, the light went out. She froze. No one was there except Rosa. The gentleman had vanished without saying a word.

The gaunt ghost of Alfred Morse Webster. *Roger Scholz.*

Rosa's entire body shivered as she tried to take in what had just happened. Her knees shook as the elevator doors opened. She hurriedly stepped on and hit the button for the upper floor. As the doors began to close, she looked up. Standing in the hallway in front of her was the same man. Only now, he looked gaunt, with dark circles under his eyes and what looked to be a trickle of fresh blood coming out of his mouth. She was too scared to cry out. She closed her eyes tight and fell to the floor, hugging her knees. She did not open her eyes until her cleaning partner, having heard her earlier scream, greeted her anxiously when the elevator doors opened on the third floor. Rosa never saw the man again.

After Rosa told her coworker what she saw, word spread. Over the next couple of weeks, Rosa said, others came to her, sharing stories about similar things that happened to them in that location: everything from doors slamming on their own to the unexplained bang of what sounded like a gunshot and lights turning on and off by themselves.

Several months after interviewing Rosa, I was able to track down a picture of Alfred. We met up once more, and I set five photographs of different gentlemen in front of her, all taken around the 1920s. I asked her if any of them looked familiar. She immediately pointed to the picture of Alfred Morse Webster and said, "I have no doubt that is him!" She had goosebumps

The grave site of Alfred Morse Webster. *Brad Donaldson.*

up and down her arms. "Even though it's been years since I saw him, I can't forget his face. He had such sad eyes."

I have stood outside this building many times at night, waiting for my ghost tour to start. While waiting patiently, I've had the feeling of being watched from the windows above. On a couple occasions, my eyes have been pulled to what I can only describe as a dark shadow moving through the unlit rooms. It is not caused by the headlights of a passing car or any other exterior light source. The form I have seen is so black, you cannot even see through it. I cannot help but wonder if Dr. Alfred Webster is watching me tell his tale to the people down below. I also wonder if the future winning bidder of this property might be getting a little something extra with their purchase.

CHAPTER 2
VICTIMS OF OBSESSION

LOCATION: 118–120 EAST FULTON STREET

Frank Hibben Stout's life started out as anything but easy. His father died right before he was born, leaving his mother, Harriet, a seamstress, solely responsible for him and his sister Nellie, who was visually impaired. Harriet did what she could, but in 1876, she brought Frank to an orphanage in hopes of finding a family to foster him. At the time, it seemed like nothing more than a miracle when a kindly farmer appeared at the institution and took a strong liking to the six-year-old boy's wit. It was with the best of intentions that Mr. Eli Hartman signed the papers and took young Frank to his house, which would now be home.

Frank fit in well with the entire family. He immediately bonded with his new foster sister Ada, who was two years his junior. They did everything together. Wherever she went, he went. As Ada began to show interest in other boys, Frank's true colors began to show. He became possessive and jealous. He had obviously developed feelings for Ada that were considered inappropriate between siblings. In 1885, the farmer passed away, and Frank was sent back to live with his mother. With financial instability looming, Ada's mother began to encourage Ada to start her own life and family.

When Ada turned sixteen, she was married in Berrien County to James McCoy on June 4, 1889. James was a thirty-two-year-old saloonkeeper who had a bad habit of drinking more alcohol than he sold. Unfortunately for Ada, she didn't discover this fact until the wedding had already taken place. She put up with his abusive ways until, in a fit of violence, James got rough and crippled their baby. She packed up and left. In 1893, Ada married

Frank Hibben Stout and Ada Mann. *From the* Grand Rapids Press, *December 11, 1915.*

engineer Charles Berkheiser and moved to Benton Harbor. The following year, they had a son named Harry.

Frank's life also continued to have its ups and downs. At eighteen years old, his girlfriend, Lillie Day, became pregnant, and they married. They had a daughter seven months later and lived in Hillsboro, Ohio. Sadly, their daughter, Hazel, died on January 28, 1894, at the age of three. While no death certificate has been found, a newspaper article published three days after her passing said that Frank had a "case of scarlet fever in his family." He and Lillie divorced six years later.

Frank met and married his second wife, Marie, in 1908. They left Ohio and moved to Grand Rapids in 1911 when Frank took a job as an estimator for the Stile's Brothers Lumber Company. They moved into a home on Adams Street SE. It was around this time that the marriage started to show signs of trouble. The stress of the new job and ongoing financial problems were too much for Frank, and he began to drink excessively. When they'd lost all their property and were down to their last dollar, Marie had had enough. She filed for divorce. Devastated, Frank begged her to stay and promised to change his ways. His company paid for him to enter a rehabilitation facility, and he cleaned up his act.

About this time, Ada filed for divorce from her second husband and moved by herself to Grand Rapids. She had heard it was a budding town full of opportunity. She found a job as a housekeeper for Dr. Groner, who lived at 112 Sheldon Avenue SE, and took up residence a block over, at 232 Sheldon.

It wasn't long before Ada began to see Frank around town. At first, she was genuinely happy to see him, a familiar face in a strange city. They were seen eating lunch together on multiple occasions, and all seemed well until a couple months in. The trouble began when Frank asked Ada for a $600 loan. If he didn't pay off the debt he owed on his home, he and his wife would lose the house. He harassed Ada until she reluctantly gave him the money. Things got worse when Ada began to date other men. Frank voiced his displeasure and began stalking Ada around town. He also began to drink heavily again. Ada did all she could to try and avoid Frank.

Marie got wind that her husband had been seen with Ada Mann around town. Although Frank told her that Ada was his foster sister, Marie did not believe him. Prior to Ada moving to Grand Rapids, Frank had never mentioned being in a foster home. Assuming her husband was being unfaithful and knowing he was back on the bottle, Marie filed for divorce again—this time with every intention of going through with it. Frank packed his belongings and relocated to the Fulton, a historic twenty-six-room boardinghouse situated at 118–120 Fulton Street. Originally constructed by the Buchanan family, prominent figures in Grand Rapids history, the house had been repurposed into a boardinghouse and medical offices. Dr. Dursum, who leased half of the space for his medical practice and sanitarium, managed one side, while the other half was run by his sister-in-law, Mrs. F.E. Bussell, as a rooming house.

Frank began to make new plans for his future. Accepting that his wife was officially done with him, he decided he would start fresh in Detroit; a bigger city meant more opportunities for success. He told Ada about his plan, and at first, she supported him. She believed a new start could be exactly what he needed to sober up and get his life together. Ada also knew that the farther away he was from her, the better. Then Frank came up with another idea. He wanted Ada to move with him and be his housekeeper. She, however, was not interested.

"Frank, I have a life here, and I'm not leaving Grand Rapids." As soon as he heard that, he lost it. He grabbed Ada by the neck and began to choke the life out of her. She fought back, ripping her clothes in the process. Ada managed to free herself from his grasp and took off running back to her

The Fulton, where Ada was murdered and Frank took his own life. *Courtesy of Sarah Boye.*

boardinghouse. Obviously flustered when she arrived, she told the other roomers, "Frank has gone crazy and is going to kill me."

The next day, Frank came to the house seeking forgiveness, but Ada refused to see him for fear of more violence. After being turned away at the door, he called and begged to speak with her, saying he was going away the next day. Again, she refused to speak with him. Two days passed, and there was no sign of Frank. Everyone assumed he had left for Detroit, but Ada was still cautious. Before she left for work on Friday morning, she penned a note saying, "Should anything happen to me, please notify my sister," and left it on her nightstand. On her way out the door, she told another boarder in her house, "Should Frank reach me today, he will surely kill me."

The city seemed quiet as Ada walked her regular route to work on Friday, December 10, 1915. She arrived at Dr. Groner's home and began to go about her daily chores. All seemed well until she started dusting the mantel in the living room. In the mirror mounted on the wall above, she caught a glimpse of Frank peeking at her through the window. She immediately went to check that the doors were locked; they were. Ada stood in the hallway, not knowing what to do. It was then that she heard someone playing with the lock and the doorknob turning. She sighed with relief when she saw it was just the other housekeeper letting herself in. Before she could shut the door, however, Frank pushed his way in. Ada's heart sank as they stood staring at each other. Seconds later, Dr. Groner arrived home and, sensing tension, asked Frank to leave. Irritated, Frank appeared to make his way back to the Fulton.

Soon after, Ada left to make a trip into town. As she hesitantly walked down Fulton Street, Frank appeared out of nowhere. He grabbed her arm and forced her, under threat, to walk to his rooming house. Once in front of the Fulton, terror gripped Ada, and she attempted to escape. She rushed into the building crying for help. She ran into the dining room where Mrs. Bussell and Dr. Dursum's wife were having tea.

"Save me! Save me!" she screamed. Frank barged into the room and yelled, "Well, I've got you, Ada!" He pulled a .38-caliber revolver out of his waistband and fired off three shots, two of which hit Ada directly in the abdomen. She sank to the floor between the two women, who by now were shrieking in fear. Frank made no sign that he even noticed them. He turned around and slowly walked up the stairs to his room. Once there, he stood in front of the mirror, pressed the gun barrel to his head and pulled the trigger. He died instantly.

When Dr. Dursum returned home from visiting a sick patient, he found chaos. Ada was rushed to St. Mary's Hospital, but it was of no use. She died from a hemorrhage without speaking another word to anyone. Both bodies were brought to O'Brien's morgue, located across the street from where the tragedy occurred.

Two of Ada's brothers came to Grand Rapids to claim her body and gave an interview to the *Grand Rapids Herald*. They said they had never heard of Frank being a foster child in their parents' home but also admitted

The tragic end. *Roger Scholz*.

they weren't a tight-knit family. The brothers conceded that the family had scattered when the children were small, and they lost track of each other. They laid Ada to rest in a cemetery near her family's childhood home in Penn Township. Her second son, Harry, whom she had all but abandoned, declined to attend her service. No further information could be found on what became of Ada's crippled child from her first marriage.

As for Frank's wife Marie, she took the news of her husband's actions calmly and denied that Frank ever borrowed money from Ada. She told a local reporter, "While I don't want to put the blame on one person, Ms. Mann had been married twice, and in both instances, had been divorced." Just how that contributed to poor Ada being shot by Marie's psychotic husband is unknown. She buried Frank in Oakhill Cemetery on the southeast side of Grand Rapids. He has no marker.

I was able to hunt down one of Frank's relatives, George Hibben. He is a master genealogist who has done an astonishing job pulling together his family's history. Not wanting to leave any stone unturned or get my facts wrong, I asked him to look over what I had written about his ancestor. I apologized in advance and forewarned him that my chapter didn't exactly show his predecessor in the best light. I was pleased when he wrote back, "I am not offended by it. Every family has a wide range of characters, some successful, creative and leaders of our country; some unable to find success, disturbed and a threat to family and friends. All their stories should be told, as you said, after it is backed up."

George shared with me that his family was well known, particularly in the eighteenth century, as being wealthy religious and business leaders in Hillsboro, Ohio. He had never heard of Frank being put into foster care but was as curious as I was about how it came about. George had copies of U.S. Census reports saying that Frank was living with his mother and sister in 1880 and 1900. We don't know for sure how long he lived with the Hartmans or exactly why he was sent away. Was George an embarrassment to his family, or was it the result of him acting off? We'll never know for sure.

The Haunting

One year after the murder and suicide, the Fulton was torn down. In its place a small, one-story building was built of brick. To this day, it seems stunted compared to the six-floor Loraine Building that sits directly to the east. Through the years, many businesses have come and gone, selling products such as medical equipment and college textbooks.

One day, as I passed by, back in the 1990s, curiosity got the best of me. I decided to go inside to see what it looked like. As soon as I entered, I could feel a heaviness in the air. I could tell someone, or something, was in that building that I couldn't see.

I walked up to the main counter, where three women stood. Two looked to be in their early twenties and continued to chat with each other. The third woman was a little bit older and greyer on top. With a friendly smile, she introduced herself as Beth and asked how she could be of help. Trying not to look too nosy, I told her I walked by their building all the time and was curious about what types of items they carried. She was cordial and told me to let her know if I had any questions. I feigned interest in their products for a couple minutes before I walked back up to the counter.

"This is quite an old building. Have any of you ever experienced anything weird here?" I had the attention of all three women now. "Like ghosts?" one asked. I nodded. Both younger women simultaneously said, "No." What they didn't see was Beth, standing behind them. Her eyes had turned big like saucers, and her head beckoned to the side for me to follow her. Across the room, she stood close and began to share her story.

"I was here one evening working on inventory and had to bring some extra stock down to the basement. As I took a step down, I looked at the bottom of the steps and saw a man standing there looking back up at me. He was drenched in some dark red substance that had to be blood." I watched goosebumps appear all over her body as she recalled what she saw. "He had no pupils. He was sopping wet in what looked like dark red blood…or tar… and all I could see was the whites of his eyes! There were no pupils! I threw the two small boxes I had in my hands at him, grabbed my purse and ran straight home. I've refused to work alone ever since."

Beth told me she had never shared her experience with anyone except her husband, who believed it was her overactive imagination. She didn't want to frighten any of her coworkers or have them think she lost her mind. Her boss assumed she no longer wanted to work nights alone for safety reasons. She didn't correct him.

I didn't discover the story about Frank Hibben Stout and Ada Mann until 2014. When I did, I immediately visited Brian's Books—the business that was there at the time—and asked the workers there the same question I had asked the ladies years before. All of them looked at me with blank stares. A couple said they would occasionally hear strange noises coming from the basement, but no one had ever seen anything (particularly the terrible apparition that Beth had described). Since most of the workers were young college students, I decided not to share the gruesome story I had uncovered about the ground they were standing on. I'd have hated for them to be uncomfortable going to work.

More recently, the building has become a popular restaurant called MeXo Tequila & Mezcal Bar. The executive chef, Oscar Moreno, is known for his passion for adding a modern touch to true Mexican dishes. One evening, while partaking of his culinary talents, I asked employees if they had ever experienced anything out of the ordinary. The waitress told me that everyone who works there knows the place is haunted, particularly the basement. They have named the ghost Charlie, and several people have seen him downstairs near what they call the chemical room. "We all feel completely creeped out down there, and we know of at least four incidents where people have seen him disappear in front of their eyes." I also spoke with the bartender, who told me he doesn't believe in ghosts but has

The Fulton Street ghost, described as dripping with a dark substance like blood or tar. *Roger Scholz.*

seen bottles and glasses move around on the bar by themselves. He also saw a glass mysteriously explode when no one was around it.

Taking things a step further, I contacted several different people who had previously lived in the Adams Street home Frank shared with his wife Marie. While some said they had never noticed anything odd, two different families reacted quite another way. The first man I spoke with was named Freddie. He immediately asked how I knew the place was haunted. He then shared that he had several paranormal experiences when living there. Unfortunately, he never elaborated more than that and soon became unreachable.

The second woman I contacted was Nadine Battles. Nadine graduated from Cornerstone University with a master's degree in counseling. It is quite

MeXo Tequila & Mezcal Bar on Fulton Street. *Brad Donaldson.*

evident that she has a good head on her shoulders. She is strong in her faith and extremely passionate about helping others. At first, I think, she was a little put off when I told her my reason for making contact. The next day, however, she shared with me that she had spoken with her children, and they all recalled events that took place while they were living in the home from 1997 until 2008.

It began with her youngest daughter, Kiera, feeling uncomfortable in the bedroom she shared with her cousin. Nadine assumed her nine-year-old, being new to the home, was afraid of the dark like a lot of children her age. At bedtime, they would close the bedroom door to block out the scary shadows in the hallway; by morning, it would unexplainably be open. It was an old house, so they figured it was from natural causes, despite it happening night after night.

Kiera had developed a nightly routine where she would close her bedroom door, change into her pajamas, shut off the light and run to her bed. One night, before she could even reach her bed, she heard the doorknob turning. Drawing the sheets over her head as quickly as she could, she lay there shaking. Slowly, she pulled the covers down and peered out toward the hallway. In the doorway was a huge black shadow. It stood as tall as the doorframe and didn't have a face. Terrified, Kiera called out to her cousin that there was a man standing in the doorway. Although Kiera was looking directly at the shadow person, her cousin was unable to see him. This startling apparition came to torment Kiera on many nights. Nadine's middle daughter, Kristen, also saw the man on multiple occasions. She had one thing going for her, however. Kristen was an extremely heavy sleeper and was very hard to wake up. Luckily for her, she slept through most of the events that occurred in the home.

In the upstairs hallway, there was another door that never seemed to stay shut. It led to the attic crawl space and continually popped open on its own—not too weird, until you consider that it only happened at night. During the day, it stayed shut fine. Whenever anyone walked by it, they felt a cold chill up their back.

Nadine's oldest daughter, Kristye, was also plagued by this unseen presence. She would hear tapping sounds on her window that would make it close to impossible to fall asleep. One night, out of frustration, Kristye yelled out, "Would you please stop it?" Immediately, the tapping stopped—never to be heard again. Unfortunately, it was replaced by other irritating antics. Her name would be called when no one was there. Her blankets were tugged from her bed when she was still awake, and her feet were tickled.

Nadine had her own harrowing experiences. She would be awakened with the feeling that something or someone was holding her down so tightly it would take her breath away. Although she could hear her children in the other rooms of the house, she was unable to call out for help. She tried to fight it but was unable to move her arms and legs. Instinctively, Nadine began to recite Psalm 23: "The Lord is my shepherd; I shall not want." Repelled, the force that held her down vanished. This happened time and time again. It became such a common occurrence that she started calling out to Jesus for help, which seemed to work quicker.

Death reaching out on Adams Street *Roger Scholz*.

One night, Nadine awoke with the feeling that someone was watching her. As she looked toward the foot of her bed, she saw a figure that appeared to be the Grim Reaper. Slowly, it raised its arm and held up three bony fingers. Mentally, Nadine had reached a breaking point. Too annoyed to be scared, she told it, "Dude, you can take your butt back where you came from, because I'm not going anywhere tonight!" She then rolled over and went back to sleep. The ghastly figure disappeared, and she never saw it again.

While the tragedy of Ada and Frank took place over one hundred years ago, it seems Frank's soul continues to linger in both of his previous homesteads. Is he stuck here out of guilt for the evil acts he committed? Did some demonic force resembling the Grim Reaper have anything to do with influencing Frank? (It had already claimed two souls; could it have been looking for a third when it showed itself to Nadine?) Either way, something sinister continues to roam Fulton Street.

CHAPTER 3

WRONG FLOOR

LOCATION: 72 SHELDON BOULEVARD SE

The date was July 2, 1917, and it was with great excitement that Mr. James Wilmer Hunter and his wife, Emma, pulled out of the driveway of 480 Morris Avenue SE for the last time. Months before, they had decided to sell their home and move downtown, and today was the day. Both were in their sixties, and the idea of not worrying about mowing lawns and maintaining a house was quite attractive. After searching for just the right place, they decided on the Hotel Browning.

James had worked for the railroad for over forty years and was the superintendent of the northern division of the Grand Rapids and Indiana Railway Company. A perk of his new home was that he could now walk to work, which was less than four blocks away.

When the Hotel Browning opened in 1917, it instantly became the latest hot spot in Grand Rapids. Hailed as the "newest fire-proof building" in town, it had its own bowling alley, billiards and pool, as well as the best café around. Out-of-towners were impressed to find that each hotel room came with its own bath, a feature that drew notable figures such as Babe Ruth and famed actor Spencer Tracy.

The six-floor brick building, located on the corner of Sheldon Boulevard and Oakes Street, was quite impressive from the outside as well. One would never know that it had already claimed one soul. A thirty-five-year-old mason named Thomas Burns had come to town from his city of Mansfield, Ohio. On July 31, 1916, he was on top of the partially built structure when he leaned over to examine cement that had recently been poured. Burns lost

Hotel Browning (*on the right*) in its heyday. *Courtesy of the Grand Rapids Public Museum Collection.*

his balance and fell ten feet, striking his abdomen on a beam. Soon after, he died from injuries sustained in the fall. Initially, his coworkers had thought he'd had a heart attack, but the coroner ruled that out during the autopsy. The official cause on his death certificate is listed as "shock and injuries falling from one floor to another on building."

The Hunters began to unload their furnishings that Monday morning. James and the hotel staff carried everything up to their new flat on the fourth floor as Emma began to unpack. They finished carrying up the last box a little after five-thirty in the afternoon. James, being a generous individual, went down to the main floor of the hotel to tip the staff that had spent their day toiling away to help him. As they thanked him, he stepped onto the elevator with another of the building's occupants, Mrs. J.B. Mooney, and the thirty-five-year-old elevator operator, John Guest. James told the operator, "Fourth floor, please." The elevator came to a stop on the third floor, where Mrs. Mooney stepped off. Evidently thinking it was his floor, Mr. Hunter attempted to step out—just as the car shot upward again. He was knocked off his feet, and his head was pinched between the floor of the elevator and the upper part of the doorframe, smashing in his skull. Horrified, the operator attempted to help the situation by reversing the direction of the lift. James's body fell out of the elevator to the third floor, where it dangled into the elevator shaft and was hit a second time as the lift came to a stop. While he was almost cut in half, the coroner found that death was instantaneous from the initial blow he received to his head.

When the hotel staff knocked on the door, Emma could tell something was wrong. Nothing could have prepared her for the horrifying story she was about to be told. Instead of starting a thrilling new chapter in their lives, her loving husband was dead. Not wanting to stay in the accursed apartment alone, Emma walked with the staff down the stairwell, to avoid the bloody scene in the elevator. Prostrated by the shock, she lay in the main sitting area sobbing and wailing for what seemed like hours.

Word reached the railway president, John Harding Page Hughart, who came running to the hotel. He stayed with Emma until arrangements were made for her to return to her home on Morris Avenue, where she was kept under the care of a nurse for months as she struggled to accept what had happened.

An inquest was held regarding the elevator mishap. The coroner's jury determined it to be an accident and recommended the Hotel Browning's elevators all be equipped with safety appliances to prevent future calamities. They also demanded that all elevator operators be instructed to call their floors and use every possible precaution to safeguard the lives of passengers. All hotels in downtown Grand Rapids quickly adapted the same procedures for the safety of their guests.

Mr. Hughart, the kind man who came to Emma's side after her husband's death, met with tragedy one month after James died. On August 16, John had spent the night at his brother's home at 302 Fulton Street (at the Lafayette Avenue intersection). Around nine-thirty in the evening, he walked into a stairway at the rear of the hall on the second floor and lost his balance. He fell to the bottom of the steep staircase and lay there unconscious until one of the servants found him. His spinal cord was damaged from the fall, leaving John paralyzed from his hips down and in unbearable pain. He succumbed to his injuries two days later.

On November 15, 1930, Emma Hunter died from interstitial nephritis (kidney trouble) after checking herself into the Kneipp Sanitarium in Rome City, Indiana. Her body was shipped to Chicago, Illinois, where she was buried beside James and the rest of her family. She never remarried.

Countless people came through the Browning's doors when it was a hotel and rentable apartments, some of whom never walked out on their own. One of the more notable occupants who died there was Emma Strahan (Emma was apparently a popular name in the early 1900s). She was seventy years old when she died in her apartment on September 22, 1917, after an illness that lasted five weeks. She was one of the founders of the D.A. Blodgett Home for Children and an active member of several clubs, including the Ladies Literary Club, located directly across the street from the Hotel Browning.

The lower level of the hotel was rented out to numerous businesses, including a medical establishment known as the Neal Institute. It was known for offering a "three-day cure for the liquor habit." The facility often had individuals go cold turkey when it came to their heroin, morphine and other addictions. Negligence charges were brought forward on more than one occasion after patients had adverse reactions to treatment.

One of the more publicized cases happened in 1915, prior to the Neal Institute moving into the new hotel. Walter Brittain, a fifty-eight-year-old farmer from Reno, Michigan, voluntarily checked himself into rehab after a fifteen-year addition to morphine. His son, Ward, was by his side the entire visit, even sleeping in the same room. Days after Walter checked in, his doctor was taken ill with smallpox and put into an isolation hospital. At that point, the proprietor of the Neal Institute, a nurse named George Quick, took charge of Walter's case. On the morning of March 24, Walter was resting when Quick administered a dose of hyoscine, which is used to calm abdominal spasms. Ten minutes later, Brittain was pronounced dead. George Quick was arrested on the charge of illegally practicing medicine and brought to the local jail. He was quite nervous about the whole situation and sure that the court would hold him accountable for the death. Before the incident could even make it to court, however, the case against him was dismissed due to an error made in the warrant when it was drawn up in the prosecutor's office. Less than two years later, under new management, the Neal Institute declared bankruptcy. The head of the institute at the time blamed Prohibition for the failure of the business, as there were "few alcoholics left" to receive treatment.

After the Neal Institute closed, the hotel carried on for many years. In 1951, the entire building was purchased by the Ferguson Hospital, known nationwide as best in class for colon and rectal surgeries. Although it was one of the top hospitals in the country, using cutting-edge methods, quite a few people died on its grounds. In 1998, a company bought the building and renovated it as studio apartments for low-income individuals with disabilities, which it remains today.

The Haunting

Over the last couple of years, I have had the pleasure of interviewing a former employee of the Ferguson Hospital, as well as several people who currently live or have lived on the premises. The one thing all their stories had in common was a woman seen walking the halls, wailing in pain and desperation.

The former employee of the Ferguson, Chris, worked there for over four years and personally saw or heard the female specter on five separate occasions. She said the first was, hands down, the most chilling. It was smack dab in the middle of a workday. Chris had been prepping examination rooms with gowns and other storable items when she heard a woman cry out in what sounded like absolute terror. She quickly poked her head out into the hallway and saw a nurse standing against the wall, hiding her face with her hands. Chris looked around and, not sensing any danger, walked up to the nurse to comfort her.

"I walked up to her to make sure she was okay, but the instant I put my hand on her shoulder, she jumped a mile high. Once she looked up and saw it was me, she hugged me tight and would not let go. She was obviously terrified. I asked her what was wrong, but she was too scared to even talk. Her lips moved, but no noise came out."

Still not knowing why her coworker was upset, Chris looked around for anything out of the ordinary. At the end of the hallway, there were two closed doors that the other nurse seemed to be staring at. The hospital had previously had issues with vagrants coming in off the streets and causing trouble. Maybe another had snuck in, threatened or scared the nurse and then shut himself into a room. That theory was quickly put to rest.

"I suddenly hear the exact same scream come from the end of the hallway and watch as the upper half of a woman floats through the door on the right. She was all gray, and I could completely make her out."

Chris described what she saw as a female with her hair loosely pulled back into a bun. Straggling strands of hair were matted on her wet, tearstained cheeks, barely covering the dark circles under her black eyes. In the bright office lights, Chris could make out veins showing through her skin, which she described as "thin, like crepe paper." Only the upper half of her body was visible—no waist, no feet—all in shades of gray.

The specter hung in the air for a moment before looking directly into the eyes of the two women. Her lips curled up into a wicked smile, exposing rotted teeth peeking out from between thin lips. She then let out another wretched wail and disappeared in front of their eyes.

The ghost of a screaming woman has been seen and heard. *Roger Scholz.*

Chris explained, "The nurse and I were shaken up and could not rationalize what we had seen. Apparently, my coworker had never even made a noise. The scream that attracted my attention had been made by the spirit as she first crossed paths with my coworker in the hallway."

As time passed and it all began to seem like a bad dream, they began to joke about what they saw as their "dirty little secret." While there were always rumors about the building being haunted, no one wanted to discuss them for fear of being judged as crazy. The spirit crossed paths with Chris on a few other occasions, but none as frightening as the first. "I heard her horrible wail on a couple different days and nights but never saw her unsightly face again, thank God."

A security guard for the Spectrum Health Medical Group building across the street came outside during one of my nightly tours to find out why a crowd was gathered in front of the building he was protecting. Once I introduced myself and explained that we were talking about the historical events and paranormal things that have happened in the building across the street, he became excited to share the experiences he has had.

Leo's job was to secure the building on the northeast side of the intersection. At the time, there was an overpass over the street connecting it to the old Hotel Browning. During his shift, motion detectors continually went off throughout the entire building, set off by something that could not be seen with the naked eye. When crossing the overpass on patrol, he would hear the whispers of unexplained voices in the corridor directly in front of him. He also heard a woman crying in the hotel, a horrible sound that he could never pin down to a living person. When I told him about the hotel's history and the legend of the crying lady, he seemed to gain a sense of relief, comforted to hear that others have experienced similar events.

My favorite—and by far the most flamboyant—tenant that I spoke with also came out in the middle of one of my tours. He was wearing a bedazzled evening gown, a blond wig, high heels and lipstick and absolutely reeked of

Hotel Browning in 2023. *Brad Donaldson.*

alcohol. Like the security guard, he was curious what we were all gathered around for. Again, I politely introduced myself, which immediately started him off on sharing his experiences. Intoxicated as he was, none of us were taking him too seriously. I gave him my card and asked him to contact me on a different day—hoping he'd go on his way. Humorously, he then followed us to the next two stops on our route. At that point, I went up to him and told him he had to go. He immediately got upset, saying, "It's because of the way I'm dressed, isn't it?" I truthfully told him, "No, I'd rock that dress too, but you didn't pay for the tour, and everyone else did." He thought that was funny and headed home. He called me the next day, and I agreed to go meet up with him.

He called himself Unique, and I was in no way let down. The guy was a trip—even sober. He walked me into the foyer of the old hotel, and although it was a little worn down, I was taken aback by the beautiful crown moldings on the walls. An intricate staircase with a natural wooden balustrade wound upward, set off by the rose-colored wall panels. Immediately, I was able to imagine what this building must have looked like in its heyday. Unique gave me a quick tour of the main areas and started to share his story. When he first moved in two years prior, he was told by a neighbor that the place was haunted by the "gray lady." He said that he rolled his eyes when he first heard this but, over the next few weeks, started to wonder, as he was told by more than one person about the experiences they had. One night, he was woken up by a woman crying and yelling in the hallway, but when he went to see who it was, the hallway was quiet and empty. The one thing that pushed him into believing, however, was what he found in the basement. Unique had a friend named John who was willing to let him borrow some books to read but said he had them stored away in the basement of the building. Together, they went down to get them, passing several rooms that Unique believed were being used for storage.

"It was freezing down there and had a really creepy vibe. I followed John, and we joked that it was the perfect spot to film a horror movie. It was funny till we went into the room where he said he had his stuff. He walked over to this wall of doors and opened one of them up. He then slid out the drawer, which looked more like a table. That's when it hit me, and I yelled, 'Hell is empty, and all the devils are here!' I took off running and didn't look back."

Unique was frightened when it hit him that the storage drawer was an old body cooler from when the room was a morgue. The table John slid out of the wall was where the hospital morticians would have placed the dead bodies.

Unique summed up his feelings about the place: "Ain't nobody getting me back down to that basement, and the next time I hear some chick crying, she best cry to someone else!"

So, who is the woman in gray? Is it Emma Hunter crying out in mourning for her husband who was taken away so suddenly? Is it one of the patients who lost their battle against drugs at the Neal Institute or some poor soul whose body was ravaged by cancer at the Ferguson Hospital? Perhaps it is some unknown personality who happened to pass through the doors only to be carried out in a body bag. Chances are we will never know.

CHAPTER 4
CRYING CLARA

LOCATION: 61 SHELDON BOULEVARD SE

In the latter part of the nineteenth century, otherwise known as the Gilded Age, most Americans still believed that a woman's place was in the home. Skill-building, beyond things like needlework, wasn't seen as necessary. To break out of their monotonous lives, many women would put their energy toward charitable works at their church or patriotic fundraising to get out of the house. But as time went on, those same women began to challenge the constraints placed on them by society. They wanted more and began to take educating themselves into their own hands. This is how the Woman's Literary Club on Sheldon Boulevard came to be.

Marion Louise Withey was one of the earliest promoters of women's clubs in our city. She was born in Vermont to the Hinsdill family on July 19, 1829. When Marion was six years old, the family moved to Grand Rapids. Ten years later, she married probate judge Soloman Lewis Withey, who was later appointed judge for the Western District of Michigan by President Abraham Lincoln. She began her philanthropic work during the Civil War, devoting all her time to getting supplies for field hospitals and the Union army. Her charitable efforts developed into the Union Benevolent Association (UBA) Training School for Nurses. She was also involved in the development of Park Congregational Church, which began as a prayer service in her father's home.

It was through Marion's efforts that Mrs. Lucinda Stone (known as Michigan's Mother of Women's Clubs) came to Grand Rapids to help formally organize a history club. Once word got out, ladies from all around town began to show interest in joining. By 1870, they had formally organized the Ladies' Literary Association. Marion was made president in 1871, the same year she worked with the board of education and the Young Men's Christian Association to form the first public library in town. In 1882, the group incorporated as the Ladies Literary Club of Grand Rapids.

In 1887, the organization had become so successful that they began to look for a location to build a stately clubhouse. Originally, they were in talks to buy the southeast corner of Fountain Street and Bostwick Avenue, where the backside of the Grand Rapids Main Public Library sits today. The owner of the land lived in the house next door and was selling the plot for extra cash. Her only stipulation was that anything they built on the land had to sit a minimum of ten feet back from the road. She loved the view looking down the hill from her front porch and didn't want anything to obstruct it. That demand made too much of the square footage unusable, so the club decided to pass. Three days later, they found the lot on Sheldon Boulevard that would soon be their new home.

William G. Robinson, the esteemed architect behind the iconic Voight House (115 College SE) and Fox House Castle (455 Cherry SE), was commissioned for the project. He designed the asymmetrical Romanesque-style meetinghouse, with impressive details such as a slate roof, for $6,000. Stained-glass windows were also added to the building, with the most remarkable, crafted by Tiffany in 1915, portraying a scene from Shakespeare's comedy *The Merchant of Venice*. A grand opening was held for the public on January 2, 1888. It came as no surprise when over one thousand of the city's most elite residents attended, and membership began to take off.

The Ladies Literary Club continued to educate and bring awareness to important issues, from politics and science to literature and art. It hosted many famous individuals, from national columnist Ann Landers to U.S. presidents Theodore Roosevelt, William Howard Taft and Woodrow Wilson. Popular figures who performed there, such as Edgar Bergen, would leave autographed photos behind, some of which still adorn the walls. When the club wasn't having meetings, it would rent out the building for events such as concerts and stage plays. In 1971, it was added to the National Register of Historic Places.

On November 16, 1912, Marion Withey suffered a cerebral embolism and passed away in her home on Cherry Street. She was eighty-three years old. She left behind a legacy of grace and compassion, having changed the lives of so many for the better.

The former clubhouse of the Ladies Literary Club. *Brad Donaldson.*

As opportunities for women became more the norm, membership began to decline. The club continued to host events to help pay for the upkeep of the building but eventually disbanded in 2005. In 2006, ownership was transferred over to Calvin College, a local Christian university. After making over $1 million in improvements to handicapped access, stage lighting and sound systems, it continued to use the building as a venue for entertainment. Eight years later, the college decided to reduce its long-term debt by selling real estate assets that weren't deemed core to its mission. This meant it was time for a new chapter for the Ladies Literary Club building.

In 2019, four investors were looking for a downtown location to create an event venue when they came across the building and purchased it for

$500,000. While still holding true to its historical significance, they did a beautiful job creating the most amazing wedding and event space, known as the Lit. One change they made was removing the downward-sloping floor in the auditorium, making the space level and more suitable for different events. This included removing the old wooden chairs that were permanently installed as theater seats in the auditorium. Over the years, small bronze plates with the names of donors to the Ladies Literary Club had been screwed into the backs of those chairs. Instead of throwing that history out the door, the new owners salvaged the placards and had them installed on the top of their new bar. The Lit specializes in hosting wedding receptions, theater performances, lectures and more.

The Haunting

The first time I stepped into the Ladies Literary Club was early in the 1990s when I was a teenager, heavy into rock bands like Ugly Kid Joe and Faith No More. I wasn't exactly thrilled when my parents bought tickets for our entire family to go see a folk singer named Christine Lavin in concert. That all changed as soon as I saw the building it was being held in; it reeked of history! As I started to go up the front steps, I felt myself getting lightheaded and immediately knew the act on stage wasn't the only thing happening in this place. We walked into a small hallway with steps that led up to the second floor on the right and a lobby to the left. Normally when our parents took us out, we would get to the venue early enough to mingle for a couple minutes. On this night, however, we were running later than usual. We were immediately greeted and asked to take our seats because the show was about to begin.

As we walked into the auditorium, I got the feeling that I shouldn't sit down yet. I told my parents I had to use the restroom and excused myself as the houselights began to go down and the show started. As the door closed behind me, I became aware of how silent and still everything seemed. I could hear a single voice in the big crowd on the other side of the door, but there was no movement in the back. I walked around the corner into the lobby. The dim lighting did nothing to make the room less creepy, as most of the illumination came from the streetlights shining through the front windows. I immediately felt drawn toward the staircase, where there was a picture of a very serious-looking Marion Louise Withey wearing a high-collar dress and spectacles. At the same time, I began to hear light footsteps coming down the stairs at a snail's pace. I remember thinking to myself, *It must be a spirit,* and I backed up toward the lobby to make room for whatever was creeping down. Suddenly, a small woman around fifty years of age, in modern-day attire, turned the corner. "Can I do something for you?" asked the lady. I let out the breath I realized I had been holding and relaxed.

"It's so dim in here I was worried I was going to fall down those steps," she said. I agreed and told her that I'd thought she was a ghost. She laughed and told me, "We've been told the place is haunted." I struck up a conversation with her, curious if she spent a lot of time in the building. She said her name was Meghan and she volunteered at a lot of the events that took place there.

"It's a great way to get out of the house and see concerts and theater for free!" Meghan said. She went on to say that her husband didn't care for such things, and she felt silly paying to go by herself. Volunteering was a win-win. I told her I loved old buildings and asked her more about her ghost comment. She immediately pointed to the picture of Marion Withey and said, "She's the one that haunts the place" and motioned me to follow her into the lobby. Meghan's job for the night was to hand out water during intermission. She offered me a full paper cup as I steered the conversation back to the ghost, asking what exactly she had heard about the haunting.

"I was told lots of people see and hear a woman crying in the building, particularly on the steps I just came down. When they try to catch her, they find nothing but a cold spot and silence. They say it's believed to be Marion Withey, one of the founders of the Ladies Literary Club." When I asked Meghan why she thought Marion would be crying, she said she didn't understand that either.

"I don't know why she would be here in the building crying. She hasn't been forgotten, and her building's still a hit! It doesn't make sense to me, but that's what they say!" Meghan finished up with a smile. At that point, I thought I had better get back to my seat before my family thought I'd been kidnapped. (Side note: I absolutely loved the concert and still listen to the witty Christine Lavin to this day! I've even gone to several of her concerts— buying the tickets on my own dime.)

Around 2012, I discovered a hilarious group of improvisational comedians known as the River City Improv. They put on shows at the Ladies Literary Club for ten dollars on Saturdays, a cheap and fun date! My husband and I went to many performances, and to his dismay, I spoke to volunteers each time I went. (While I don't get embarrassed asking strangers about ghosts everywhere I go, he still cringes.) Most had heard the place was haunted but

The ghost of crying Clara has been seen on the back steps. *Roger Scholz.*

had never experienced anything. Then there was one man named Tyler who told me he literally stumbled across the spirit on a Saturday afternoon.

"I was in the auditorium when I heard a woman crying. It was muffled, like from a television or something. I ignored it at first, but it kept getting louder. When my curiosity got the best of me, I followed the sound to the staircase and looked up. There was a woman sitting there with her head in her hands, crying. She looked like a legit person! After a couple seconds, she looked up with these big tearful eyes and poof! Gone! Completely trippy!" I asked if he thought it was Marion, but he didn't know who I was talking about. Before we left that night, I brought him over to Marion's picture and showed him. He tilted his head and took a close look before he started to say, "No. Her face is different. The woman I saw looked younger and had braids in her hair."

Something didn't sit well with me. I struggled to understand why Marion Louise Withey would be hanging out at her old building that was still such a success. She had done so much good in her life; she couldn't possibly feel like she had more to accomplish, leaving her spirit stuck here in some form of purgatory. So I began my search. After countless hours of paging through newspapers, I discovered a woman who seems to be a more likely suspect in the haunting.

Clara C. Greene was born in 1848 in New York. She was raised by her mother, Sophia, and they were extremely close. Believing a good education was key to success, Sophia made sure her daughter received the finest schooling available. At the age of twenty-five, they moved together to Grand Rapids, where Clara was quickly able to secure a job in the local school system. All was going well until her mother unexpectedly passed away in 1885 of an unknown cause. That seemed to be a turning point in Clara's life, as many said she never fully recovered from the shock of losing Sophia. She didn't just lose a mom but also her best friend. After seven years, Clara left the school system and began to tutor students at her home because of what she called her "declining health." Being financially well-to-do, Clara was able to immerse herself in activities at the Ladies Literary Club, trying to forget her immense loss. Over the years, she held many different roles, including corresponding secretary and chairman. She was known for her informative presentations to the members of the club, including one on the Spanish Theater in 1900. Clara was also an active member of St. Paul's Episcopal Church.

On Thursday, July 2, 1903, Clara Greene left her home on Scribner Street for what would be the last time. The scorching temperature was in the nineties, and everyone seemed to be looking for shade and cool spots. Despite the weather, Clara wore a black wool skirt, a white linen shirt and a black hat. She was last seen by neighbors when she stopped at their farmhouse to borrow a small pail of drinking water. From there, she vanished.

By Saturday, her friends had put an ad in the *Evening Press* stating they were anxious to know of her whereabouts. It wasn't until nine days later that two young ladies walking through the woods by Walker Avenue came across a body in a bad state of decomposition. Although Clara's corpse was lying in the underbrush, the summer heat had made it unrecognizable; only her outfit helped identify her. Coroner LeRoy was notified and quickly shared his opinion that her death was a suicide. At the scene, he found small white papers and a cup near her body that showed where and how the poison had been taken. An autopsy confirmed his suspicions, as a large quantity of strychnine was found in Clara's stomach.

Once her friends found out she was dead, they began to share how Clara had been extremely depressed and convinced herself that she was losing her mind. For months, she had been saying she was ill and had a terrible foreboding that she was going insane. While a suicide note was never found, Clara had left an updated version of her will out on a table in her home. Most of her estate was left to her family, but she also bequeathed a large sum of money to the Ladies Literary Club, a place that meant so much to her. Clara asked for her remains to be cremated and buried with those of her mother in New York. Although temporarily housed in Oakhill Cemetery of Grand Rapids, Clara's body was eventually laid to rest with her mother's in the family plot at Riverview Cemetery in Oxford, New York.

The specter that has been seen and heard at the Ladies Literary Club appears to be a residual manifestation and nothing to be afraid of. Unlike spirits who interact with objects and people, residual hauntings are imprints left behind on the environment where a traumatic or emotionally charged event took place. Clara spent a lot of time at the location when she was at her lowest, in emotional agony. While we still don't understand why, when the environment is right, it appears these moments can be captured and played over and over. Some believe these imprints don't even involve the souls of the dead and that they are more of a "moment in time" stuck on repeat. This would mean Clara's spirit is not stuck in the building or even aware of any living observers. The bright side of all this is that with all the love, laughter and good times that have been had in this building, as well as all the wonderful new memories being made by the Lit, the positive energies should overwrite Clara's sad moments in no time. Here's to hoping both remarkable women are resting with the angels.

CHAPTER 5
THE GOOD, THE BAD AND THE DEAD

LOCATION: 118 COMMERCE AVENUE SW

The city of Grand Rapids was officially established in 1850 with an approximate population of 2,700 living in less than six square miles. Within seven years, the city had grown to twice its original size and become a desired location for immigrants. One of those immigrants who left an indelible mark on the city was Henry J. Heystek.

Henry was born in the Netherlands in 1861 and traveled to the United States with his parents at the age of ten. When he first set foot in this country, he knew little English. At the prompting of his mother, he began school and realized the only way he was going to be successful was to learn more and learn it quickly. Within his second school year, he had already completed the eighth grade.

Sadly, Henry lost his mother in July 1877 and his father five months later. At only fifteen years old, he was orphaned and left to fend for himself. Believing college to be financially out of the picture, he began to work at a paint and wallpaper store operated by H.M. Goebel on Canal Street. Making $2 a week, he began to save his money until, at twenty-two years old, he had saved $900 and made enough connections to be able to strike out on his own.

Henry formed a partnership with his friend C.L. Harvey, and together, they opened their own painting and wallpaper establishment on Ottawa Street, named Harvey & Heystek. (The business sat on a lot that is now the back side of the Grand Rapids Art Museum.) Their company flourished and moved to a bigger and better location at Campau and Louis Street. Thirteen years later, Harvey retired and sold his interest to Heystek, who continued to expand and grow the business.

Henry made it his mission to invest in the area around Commerce Street. Though close to downtown, it was still a dirt road, with sketchy buildings and even sketchier people. Seen through Henry's eyes, however, the land was invaluable. He purchased several lots and preached to other business owners about the potential of the location. As he brought new life into the area, they were compelled to listen. Before long, the road was paved with bricks, and beautiful new buildings were going up left and right. It gained the reputation of a sort of "business highway."

The one thing missing in Grand Rapids at that point was a banquet and convention hall. Henry got the idea to build a high-grade roller rink that could also be used for large meetings or parties. As with all his ideas, it was a great success.

The Coliseum officially opened its doors in November 1910. It cost $350,000 to build and could seat approximately 3,500 people. The building itself was quite impressive. The ornate arch on the front stretched across a large portion of the façade. The inside was thirteen thousand square feet and could accommodate up to 800 skaters at one time. The sloping roof rose thirty-two feet in the air. The convention hall was consistently booked, resulting in Henry purchasing the lot directly to the south in 1911 to expand. The acquisition increased seating by 4,500.

As far as the roller-skating rink, it became *the* place to be. Henry hired an eight-piece orchestra to play each night it was not booked for an event and brought in big names to keep the crowds coming back. Harley Davidson was a famous roller-skating and ice-skating champion known around the world. He came to Grand Rapids many times to perform at the Coliseum. (One side note: He was born in 1871, long before William S. Harley and the three Davidson brothers—Walter, Arthur and William—combined their talents to create the Harley-Davidson Motor Company. The name is just coincidental.)

The Coliseum hosted another famous name multiple times: Alice Teddy, a 215-pound roller-skating bear. She had been found in the Siskiyou Mountains by a man named George B. Crapsey. Once he brought her home, he found that when he skated, she would try to imitate him. For giggles, he fitted her up with roller skates. Before long, she was gliding around wearing a skirt and carrying a parasol. She would shake hands and give hugs and especially enjoyed challenging humans. She would race them in roller derbies and wrestling matches. Sellout crowds appeared every time she was in town.

The original entrance to the Coliseum. *Brad Donaldson.*

On January 22, 1912, the *Evening Press* published an article titled "Not Very Serious." It informed everyone that Henry was confined to his house on Paris Avenue with an attack of indigestion that was not considered critical. Imagine everyone's surprise when two days later, they published another article stating the exact opposite.

Henry unexpectedly passed away at the age of fifty on January 23 from pneumonia. Sensing his death was on the horizon, he had his will revised. In addition to leaving large sums of money to his family, he also bequeathed sizable donations to eight public and charitable institutions around the city, including hospitals, orphanages and the Salvation Army.

Despite being associated with so many fond memories, the land around the Coliseum saw its fair share of sadness as well. The gloomiest story was that of the Santman family. They lived in a small boardinghouse that stood to the north of the Coliseum (the current location of the Pyramid Scheme's parking lot).

Charles Santman's life seemed filled with tragedy. He was born in a small town in Ohio. Misfortune first struck his life when he was seventeen. While walking on the local tracks, he was hit by a train, leaving him with a fractured skull. To save his life, doctors had to insert a silver plate into his head. People who knew him closely said he acted a little off after the accident.

In 1905, Charles got married, and he and his wife, Mary, moved to Grand Rapids in 1907 to start a family. At that time, work was scarce in the city, but Charles had a strong work ethic. He started his own business hauling ashes for neighbors and soon had a long route of consistent customers. Charles spent more than his fair share of money on alcohol, and his drinking only got worse when tragedy struck again—and again—and again—in 1914.

The year began with all four of Charles and Mary's children coming down with the measles. On February 6, two days after his first birthday, their son Alton passed away from pneumonia. As expected, the parents were bereaved; Charles turned to alcohol to dull the pain. One month later, his three-year-old son, Karl, became ill and lost his battle with typhoid.

The death of his children drove Charles to act irrationally. At one point during a drinking binge, he threatened to kill his wife and remaining two children, Weltha (eight years old) and Dorothy (four years old). This threat was not taken lightly, as he was already on probation for assault and battery from a previous beating he gave to Mary. The situation got so bad that Mary cautioned little Dorothy to remain near the door when her father came home "in a mood" so the child would be able to take flight quickly if necessary.

Charles's breaking point came one month later when Weltha was stricken with typhoid fever and admitted to the hospital in critical condition. On Monday, April 6, he visited his daughter at the hospital, then headed home to talk to his wife. He told her to prepare to move to a new house; the memories in their current home were too painful to bear. He asked her to take little Dorothy and go gather boxes from local businesses so they could pack. She did as he asked. When they returned, Charles was gone. Mary assumed he went out to meet up with some friends and drink.

Late the following morning, the police received a call that Charles was drunk and lying in the alley behind the Coliseum. This was not the first time he had been found in this position. They arrived at the scene to find that instead of a wine bottle next to his body, there was an empty bottle of chloroform. Charles had apparently tried to take his own life by drinking the contents and was in a coma. He was rushed to St. Mary's Hospital and had his stomach pumped, but the damage was too severe. His liver was in a state of toxic hepatitis, and he died soon after without regaining consciousness.

Thankfully, the Social Welfare Association took pity on the family and helped them move to a new home. Mary qualified to receive a wife's pension that helped her support her family. Weltha eventually recovered.

Another death occurred on March 14, 1917. On that day, the ABC Bowling Tournament took place in the main area of the Coliseum. One of

Above: The alley, located behind the Coliseum. *Brad Donaldson.*

Left: The spot where Charles Santman drank a bottle of chloroform. *Brad Donaldson.*

the laborers was a thirty-two-year-old man named Bobby McGrath, who was known to always have a smile on his face. On that day, however, he was not feeling well. Not wanting to be a nuisance, Bobby unsteadily walked out of the big hall to one of the smaller rooms on the south side of the building. There, he spread out newspapers on the floor and laid down to rest. He was soon found by his boss, C.J. Whitrock, who tried to comfort his employee by covering him up with a coat. Leaning over him, he noticed Bobby's face was turning dark purple. An ambulance was called, and he was driven to St. Mary's Hospital. When he came through the emergency entrance, the first nurse who saw him said, "He's gone." A friend and fellow pinsetter later discovered that Bobby had a bad heart. He had been in the Canadian army but failed the final health examination and was released on medical discharge. His body was shipped back to his hometown in Pennsylvania for burial, paid for by the American Bowling Congress.

The Haunting

I discover most of the locations I know of as haunted quite by accident. A couple years ago, I went into the Lantern Coffee Bar & Lounge after getting out of a meeting. After ordering the biggest chai latte I could get my hands on, I sat down in a comfortable-looking chair at the bottom of a small staircase. A man who looked to be in his mid-thirties sat across from me drinking coffee with a newspaper in his lap. It was the first time I had been in the building, and I was intrigued by the old brickwork. My appreciation must have been obvious by my face, as he said, "You can feel the history in the walls, huh?" Before you know it, we were talking about how the place had a cool historic vibe, and he said those words that immediately grab my attention: "You know, the building's haunted."

I immediately asked him why he thought that, and he shared with me that he had a friend who lived on an upper floor, and he'd "seen things." After telling him I wrote about ghost stories in the city, he laughed. "Well, my name is Dean, and you can put me in your next book."

Jennifer, a woman Dean had been seeing off and on for the past couple of years, lived upstairs in the Grand Central Lofts. He told me the exposed brickwork extended upstairs and her apartment had a cool vintage feel to it. "The first time I came over, I thought the place was great. It reminded me of a loft I had in Chicago a couple of years ago, so it felt like home."

The ghost of Charles Santman. *Roger Scholz.*

Dean went on to tell me about a time that he and Jen were supposed to meet friends for a concert at the Van Andel Arena at six thirty. Since Jen had to work, Dean offered to get dinner ready before she got home. "From the second I let myself into her place with the key she gave me, I felt like I was being watched. I've never had that feeling before."

Intent on making spaghetti, Dean filled a large cooking pot with water and set it on the stove. When he turned the pilot on, he felt an unexplained breeze hit him from out of nowhere. Despite no fan being on, the flame danced like an unseen mouth was blowing on it. Trying to figure out the cause, Dean leaned over to take a closer look.

"I noticed in the reflection of the steel pot that a figure was standing behind me. I saw it step away as I turned my head around, but nothing was there." Immediately, the flame started to act normally.

At this point, Dean told himself it had to be his imagination—until he went to plug in his cell phone. "Jen has a small table in the entrance where she keeps a charging station. When I went to plug my phone in, I glanced in the mirror on the wall and saw the gaunt face of a man standing behind me. He wore a faded brown derby hat, and his face looked as if he were wincing in pain. I freaked out!"

Dean ran out of the apartment as fast as his feet could carry him. He left the water boiling and Jennifer's apartment unlocked and waited for her outside. Luckily, she got home soon after, and they went back up to the apartment together. She thought it was hilarious that Dean was so jumpy as she listened to him tell his tale. Her entire attitude changed, however, when Dean described the man staring back at him in the mirror. While Jennifer was not one to believe in the afterlife and had never seen a spirit in the apartment, she repeatedly had the same dream in which she woke up to find

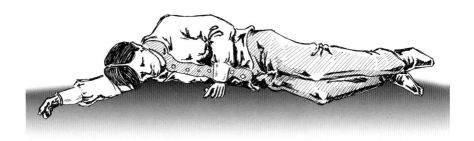

The mysterious spirit of Bobby McGrath. *Roger Scholz.*

a man wearing a brown derby hat staring down at her in bed. He whispered, "Is it you?" and then vanished.

Another renter I spoke to resides on the second floor toward the rear of the building. His windows look out on the alley where Charles poisoned himself. This renter did not want me to use his name but shared with me that on several occasions, he had seen the apparition of a man wearing a brown hat, brown pants and a white "wifebeater" sleeveless shirt with suspenders.

"On the back stairwell, I would unlock the door and start the climb up the steps to my apartment. In front of me, I would see the backside of a man turning to start the next set of steps. I would not hear the doorknob turn or the door open or close at the top, but when I got up there seconds later, he would be gone. Vanished."

Back in 2018, a lovely lady named Jill asked if she could share her Coliseum story with me after my tour one night. It is important to note that on my tour, I only tell the story of Charles Santman, for time's sake. So, I was in awe when Jill shared her tale.

"In the sixties, I worked as a secretary for a firm that was considering investing in the building. After my boss and I went in to look around with a real estate agent, I realized I left a folder in my car and went to grab it. As I walked out, I noticed a man lying on the floor by an old exit door, in the fetal position." As she said this, she lifted her hands up toward her face, as if she could still see how he was lying.

When I asked what he looked like, Jill continued, "He was nicely dressed in a button-down shirt, and his hair was perfectly parted to the side. I stopped and asked if he was okay. He never looked up but said, 'I just need a moment to rest.' I sighed and went on my way, thinking how odd he was to lie down right there. When I came back in, he was gone. I asked the man showing us around if the gentleman was okay, but he had no idea who I was talking about and said nobody else was in the building. I am wondering if it could have been Charles Santman!" I went on to tell Jill about the pin boy who spent his last moments in the building. I believe it was the spirit of Bobby McGrath that Jill encountered.

Who exactly is haunting the buildings around the Coliseum? Could it be Henry Heystek stopping by to check on his investment properties? Perhaps pinsetter Bobby McGrath is only now awakening from his "quick rest." Or is it the spirit of Charles, pathetically reliving the moments of tragedy that haunted him in life? Maybe the next tenants will be able to shed some light in the future.

CHAPTER 6

BUCK UP, DAD

LOCATION: 400 BLOCK OF LYON STREET AND COLLEGE AVENUE NE

The morning of April 4, 1940, started out as just another day in Los Angeles for grocery store manager F. Barton Davis. He kissed his wife, Lolita, goodbye in the wee hours of the morning, before any of the children woke up, and headed to work. He had only been there for a couple hours when the phone rang. When Bart answered it, he heard his eleven-year-old daughter, Chloe, on the other end. "You'd better come home right away," she declared. Before he could ask any questions, Chloe hung up.

Bart was a native of Concordia, Kansas, but had moved to Grand Rapids, where he met and fell in love with Miss Lolita D. Bjorkman. Lolita had attended Fountain Street School in her younger years and graduated from Central High School in 1922. They married in December 1926 and had three girls, Chloe, Daphne (ten years old) and Deborah Ann (seven years old). Bart was the manager of a Kroger grocery store at Wealthy Street and Eastern Avenue before the family left Grand Rapids in the early summer of 1937. They lived in South Haven for a short time before finally settling down in Los Angeles, California. There, they were blessed with a little boy, Marquis, whom they called Mark. Lolita was an amazing mother. She was always reading books to improve her relationships with the children, and her kids did everything she asked of them.

After the unusual phone call, Bart rushed home. He arrived to find his daughter Chloe sitting on the front steps, as if she was ready to go somewhere. She was in clean clothes, and her hair was brushed. Chloe looked at her father and said, "You'd better go into the house." Trying the doorknob, he

Lolita Bjorkman Davis in happier times. *From the* Grand Rapids Press, *April 5, 1940.*

found it locked. With his key, he opened the door and walked into a bloody nightmare he would never be able to forget.

The horrified father went from room to room, seeing the carnage that had once been his family home. He found the body of his wife on a burned daybed mattress in the hallway, her hair scorched off and her head unrecognizable from hammer blows. Dark red blood was spattered everywhere from her wrists, which had been slashed with a razor. White feathers littered the crime scene, beaten haphazardly out of the mattress. Three-year-old Mark was lying in the doorway to the kitchen next to Daphne, both beaten about the head. Lastly, Bart found Deborah Ann dead in the bathtub.

Bart ran out the front door screaming, "I no longer have anything to live for!" Little Chloe calmly rose from the steps and said, "Buck up, Dad! You mustn't get excited. Come on, let's go for a walk." When the police arrived, they were stunned by the gruesome scene that greeted them inside. Lolita and Mark were quickly pronounced dead. Daphne and Deborah were transported to the hospital, but nothing could be done for them. Being the only surviving member of the family, Chloe was instantly the primary suspect in the killings. While her father, Bart, had literally collapsed in agony, Chloe shed no tears. She was brought to the Police Emergency Hospital and found to have a minor head wound and blisters all over the palms of her hands.

Captain Edgar Edwards of the Los Angeles Police Department's Homicide Squad began his investigation, taking particular interest in Chloe's calm, unemotional responses. Instead of being an emotional wreck, she was lying in bed with her hands folded behind her head when he walked in. For the next twelve hours, she would tell and retell the exact same story. Chloe said she woke up to find both Daphne and Deborah Ann dead, beaten by a claw hammer in the hands of their mother. Her brother was close to death and in pain, so Lolita told Chloe to put him out of his misery, which she did with three blows to the head. Her mother said demons were coming for them all and she was trying to save the children from suffering.

Lolita then made her daughter drag a mattress into the hallway, where she sat down, cut her wrists and lit herself on fire. When that didn't kill her instantly, she told Chloe, "I've killed them; now you kill me." Always one

Marquis (three), Chloe (eleven), Daphne (ten) and Deborah Ann (seven) Davis. *From the Grand Rapids Press, April 5, 1940.*

to listen to what she was told, Chloe hit her mother over fifty times before Lolita took her last breath. Chloe then went into the bathroom, cleaned herself up and went to her neighbor, Mrs. Randolph, to call her dad.

Once Chloe made the phone call to her father telling him to come home, Mrs. Randolph asked if everything was okay. Chloe responded, "Everything's okay. I won't say anything till Daddy gets here. It's something so terrible you'll probably read all about it in the newspapers."

During the entire interview, the only time Chloe showed any type of emotion was when those questioning her implied she was lying. Otherwise, she remained calm, cool and collected. Despite Captain Edwards insinuating she was responsible for the mess, Chloe would not be rattled, and at one point she yelled at him, "You can't make me confess! I didn't do it!" After the long interview, Chloe was transported to a juvenile detention facility, where it was noted on her admissions sheet that she was to be charged with murder. When offered dinner, she asked for a big steak and a bottle of beer. When given just a steak with no beer, Chloe boasted that she liked beer and had split one with her mother only a few days prior.

The following morning, the police took Chloe and her father back to the scene of the crime for a walkthrough. Chloe smiled and waved when she saw her neighbors, some of them classmates, standing on the lawn of the Davis residence. Completely unaffected by the grotesque scene before her, Chloe walked from room to room nonchalantly retelling the story of what had happened not twenty-four hours prior. As Bart listened to his only remaining daughter tell the story, he began to sob, "Oh my poor baby! You can't blame her! She's just as innocent as the other children! She only did what she was told to do." He then admitted, "I knew something was wrong."

Barton blurted out that his wife's mind was tortured, and she had been acting peculiar prior to the tragedy. Two weeks before, he woke to find her sitting up in bed smoking a cigarette. She said she had a terrible confession to make: an evil spirit was creeping up on them, and she was waiting for it. Alarmed, he brought Lolita to a psychiatrist the very next day. They went in for a lengthy appointment that seemed to help her. As they drove home, Lolita said she felt "as though a terrific burden had been lifted." Unfortunately, Lolita soon began to talk of the demons again. She also asked her husband where she could purchase chloroform because she wanted to pour it over the children's faces so their "pain could be eased." She even went so far as to ask Bart to help her commit suicide. She begged him to prove his love by locking her inside the family automobile and piping carbon monoxide into it with a hose. Realizing the one visit to the psychiatrist did nothing, Bart tried to get Lolita to go back, but she refused. She would only agree to see a family doctor, who ran tests on her and found that she was anemic. He gave her a shot and sent her home.

Captain Edwards followed all the leads and discovered that Bart was telling the truth. All the doctors vouched for the problems Bart was having with his wife. Those who knew Chloe came to her defense as well, stating that she was a sweet young girl and a good student who'd shown no signs of violence in the past. Once the crime scene report came in, Captain Edwards finally relented. All the fingerprints and footprints left behind at the scene matched the story that Chloe had told. There was more than enough evidence to prove that her mother had massacred the family and ordered Chloe to "finish the job." Soon, Chloe was released on probation to her dad for one year, and all other charges were dropped.

Chloe and her father moved to Ohio, where they began a new life. At twenty-two, she married Robert Dietz, but they divorced after having a son, Gary Alan. Chloe became an accomplished artist, violinist and fencer. Her father, Barton, passed away in 1956, taking away the one constant support she had in her life. In 1962, Chloe married a man named Ross Lewton from Indiana. There, she owned and operated a successful beveled glass studio known as the Bevelry in Indianapolis. She divorced Ross in 1986 and soon married Philip Blumenthal. Soon after their honeymoon, Chloe found out she had adenocarcinoma of the lung. Four months later, she passed away at home at the age of fifty-eight.

The Haunting

When I was a teenager, I had a couple of friends who went to Central High School. One night, a bunch of us were hanging out in the field behind the school when I brought up the topic of ghosts. From where we were sitting, we could see the backside of the infamously haunted Phillips Mansion that is located on Prospect Avenue. Other teens who were there talked about how the high school was haunted by a woman looking for her child. They said she could be seen all over the neighborhood wailing for her baby. Frankly, it sounded like the typical urban legend. I was surprised they didn't say she was wearing white, as that's usually how the story goes. I didn't hear any other stories about this woman for a couple years, until I went to Grand Rapids Community College in 1994.

There, I met a woman named Sarah in my biology class. Like Lolita, she had graduated from Central High School (now known as Innovation Central High School) and was so excited when I told her I was a history buff with a passion for ghost stories. Her eyes lit up, and she said, "I cannot wait to tell you what happened to me!" Sarah was a popular girl in high school. She joked that she constantly had a boyfriend but burned through them like candles. She began to share her story of a bleak, rainy Thursday when she was waiting for her current boyfriend in the hallway of the high school.

"I was sitting on the floor with my back against the wall. The place was close to being completely cleared out, but Mike had missed school the day before and was doing a makeup test, and I told him I'd wait for him." The entire building was close to empty, and Sarah jumped when the door slammed shut behind the last person to leave. It was then that she began to hear murmuring. Sarah looked down the hall toward the voice and saw a woman standing in a classroom doorway about ten feet away. Sarah described the woman: "She was wearing a blue dress with little flowers on it and was really pretty. She had dirty blond hair, big eyes and dimples." The

Lolita's high school. *Brad Donaldson.*

lady started to walk down the hall toward Sarah. As she got closer, Sarah was able to make out what she was whispering. She kept repeating, "Where are they?" over and over again. The lady gave off an extremely creepy energy, and Sarah felt uneasy.

"The sight of this chick made my stomach drop. Something was off. When she was about four feet away from me, she turned and looked directly at me, and I saw blood start to drip out of her eyes. I remember thinking, *Oh heck no!* as I stood up and started to run. I flung the door open and looked to see if she was following, but she stayed in the same spot. But her face…Her entire face had changed into something that looked like it'd been dead for years. Flaky, putrefied and nasty! I remember screaming as I ran out onto the front walk of the school and then hiding behind a tree until Michael came out and was able to grab my things." Sarah told her parents what happened at school when she got home. Her dad laughed at her and told her she needed to get more sleep. Her mom said she believed her but acted uncomfortable about the entire situation. Sarah assumed her mom thought she was making it all up.

"I absolutely hated going to school after that! It took everything in me to open the door and walk in that hallway the next morning. I was so scared but convinced myself I had to have imagined it." Though Sarah felt like she was being watched for days after that, she never saw the woman again.

The ghost of Lolita has been seen roaming her former neighborhood. *Roger Scholz.*

Several weeks later, Sarah's mom was waiting for her in the car after practice. Sarah noticed she caught her mom off guard when she opened the passenger-side door. Her mom jumped a mile, grabbed her chest and immediately started to cry. When Sarah apologized for scaring her and asked what was wrong, her mom finally confessed: "I've seen that same lady in the blue dress you spoke of when I was a sophomore, twenty-plus years ago!" Her mother went on to say she was supposed to meet a teacher regarding homework assignments she had missed in a classroom on the third floor of the school. When she walked in, the teacher wasn't there yet, but she saw the back of another student—or so she thought—sitting in the front row. Her mom stood around in the doorway for a moment or two but finally decided to take a seat and wait. She walked toward the front of the room and was starting to ease into a chair when the student sitting in the front row turned her head to look in her direction.

"All my mom could say was she saw the face of the living dead. She hightailed it out of there and never told a living soul what she saw. That's why she got so upset when I told her what I saw. She had convinced herself she must have been dreaming it all," Sarah said.

After hearing Sarah's story, I began to dig into the archives to unearth what I could find about the location on which the two schools reside. The first secret I discovered was that prior to Fountain Street School (now known as the Grand Rapids Montessori Public School), the location used to be the Grand Rapids Orphan Asylum in the 1800s. In the early 1900s, it was turned into a nursing school, and it eventually served as a hospital for the wounded during the Civil War. It became the Union Benevolent Association (UBA) Hospital, until it was torn down and the elementary school put up in its place. I found a listing of the teachers who worked at the school and mailed out letters to them asking if they had ever seen or heard anything out of the ordinary on-site. Not really expecting a response, I was pleasantly surprised several weeks later when I received a letter back. It was from a teacher who asked me to remain anonymous if I ever shared her story.

One late afternoon, I was sitting at my desk grading papers when I noticed movement out the corner of my eye. When I looked up, I saw a woman with light-colored hair walking quickly back and forth outside the windows. She seemed to be ranting about something, but I couldn't make out what she was saying. After a minute or so, she stopped and cupped her hands to the window to try to see inside. I waved when she saw me. She smiled, threw her head back and raucously started laughing. Then she started pacing back and forth again. Feeling something was off with her, I thought I should probably tell others in the school she was out there. But as I walked toward the hallway, I remembered one thing. While I was on the main floor, the windows were about eight feet off the ground. There was no way she could be walking "outside" the windows. I looked back toward her, and she was cupping her hands to the window again, staring straight at me with a smile I can only describe as disturbed. She again started laughing hysterically and then disappeared in front of my eyes. To this day, I'm not sure why I saw what I did. I have no idea who or what it was, but pray I never see anything like it again.

Could this mysterious woman be Lolita? Looking into her past, I found she was born in 1903 in Chicago, Illinois, to a couple who had come over from Sweden. By the time she was a teenager, they had moved to Grand Rapids and taken up residence across the road from the school on Lyon Street. They lived in several different homes, but they were all next door to each other at 410, 459, 440 and 445 Lyon Street (the latter being where Lolita lived prior to marrying Bart). All the homes were eventually demolished, leaving behind the parking lot you see today. In addition to

The school that three of the Davis children attended. *Brad Donaldson.*

living directly next to the two schools, Lolita attended both, as did three of her children prior to the tragedy.

Being that Lolita spent so much time and energy in this constricted area, it isn't impossible that she may have left a piece of herself there. Although the tragedy occurred across the United States, Lolita's ghost may have come back to the place where she was the happiest and made the fondest memories. She had warned Bart that an "evil spirit was creeping up" on them. Was this a case of mental illness on her part, or could Lolita see and sense something no one else could? Who is to say that an evil spirit didn't invade Lolita's body, making her harm her children? Maybe that same spirit then jumped into Chloe to finish off the job, leaving Chloe to feel no guilt on her part when it exited. Urban legends usually grow from the smallest seed of truth. In this case, a woman is wandering the block where the schools are located, crying out for her child. Sarah heard the lady ask, "Where are they?" Could Lolita eternally be looking for the children she lost? I pray that she and the entire family have found peace.

CHAPTER 7

DEAD MAN'S ROW

LOCATION: JEFFERSON AVENUE SE

The first several blocks of Jefferson Street SE harbor more grim stories than the average block around town. It is for that reason that I began to call them Dead Man's Row on my tour. In 1899, a man was found dead in bed, his pillow splattered with blood and eight whiskey bottles surrounding him. The following year, a professor was found in his bathtub, literally parboiled from spending hours in scalding water. His brother lay dead in the next room, covered in boils. To this day, their deaths are attributed to unknown causes. In 1911, a popular hotel, known as the Wellington, was sold to two doctors. They continued to operate the upper floors as a hotel for out-of-towners, while the lower levels were used as a sanitarium for the dying: the Burleson Hotel and Sanitarium. The unusual stories go on and on.

In the middle of this area, on the corner of Jefferson Avenue and State Street, stands the original Grand Rapids Public Museum. In 1854, several civic leaders, including John Ball (the man best known for donating forty acres of land that became the park and zoo on the northwest side of town), organized a group known as the Grand Rapids Lyceum of Natural History. Members were able to foresee that items they had sitting on their shelves at home would be important to share with future generations. They put together what they called the Cabinet of Curiosities. In 1868, they merged with a local group of high school students called the Grand Rapids Scientific Club and formed the Kent Scientific Institute, which officially displayed its collection at Central High School. As interest in the assortment grew, it became evident that a new, permanent home would be needed. In 1903, the board of education purchased a three-story redbrick home owned by lumberman Nelson Howlett as the collection's first "permanent" location. The museum continued to acquire items—such as Finny, a seventy-six-foot whale skeleton, in 1905. It was so large, it had to be housed in a barn across the street. Another impressive purchase was in 1909, when an Egyptian mummy named Nakhte-Bastet-Iru was brought in with accompanying treasures. Nationally, the museum began to earn a name for itself. During the Great Depression, in 1937, President Franklin D. Roosevelt signed a Works Progress Administration (WPA) grant to build a new home for the institution. The purpose of the WPA was to supply jobs to the unemployed in the United States while simultaneously building up public infrastructure. They tore down the old Howlett home and constructed a new building on the same site. On June 12, 1940, the doors opened to the brand new Grand Rapids Public Museum.

When I bring up the old museum on my tour, it's easy to tell who from the older generations remembers visiting there. Their eyes instantly light up,

The Grand Rapids Public Museum on Jefferson Avenue. *Courtesy of the Grand Rapids Public Museum Collection.*

and they start to shout out all the displays that continue to live on in their memories. The front doors were at street level and led into a huge hall with grand stairways and ornate columns. Large wings expanded out on the sides, each dedicated to its own subject, from rocks and minerals to mammals. Stunning dioramas lined the walls, showing scenes such as Native Americans hunting buffalo or wolves stalking their prey. Upstairs, there was a wall that showed each stage of pregnancy with real fetuses, a somber but moving way to see how babies developed in their mother's womb.

As visitors walked deeper into the building, wooden sidewalks transported them back in time to Gaslight Village. Meticulously re-created to look like a street in Grand Rapids in 1890, the road was lined with shops: a general store, a doctor's office, a gunsmith. Actual gaslighting, as well as several mannequins, added to the unintentional creep factor. A large horse and streetcar stood on the brick-paved road as birds chirped up in the dark sky and muffled voices played as background noise. Once through the old town, after a quick trip to the vending machine in the small break room, you would stumble upon a giant spinning globe outside of the Roger B. Chaffee Planetarium, named after our hometown astronaut who lost his life in the *Apollo I* disaster. Upstairs in the East Building was fashion from throughout the years, as well as toys. It would literally take days to get through this place and take it all in.

For years, the museum continued to be a popular place to visit, drawing people from all over. But a collection that began over 120 years ago needs space; storage again became an issue. This prompted a new facility to be built on the west bank of the Grand River in 1994. The old building on Jefferson Avenue, once the pride of the city, was forgotten. It would occasionally open for one-off events, such as the Grand Rapids Art Prize competition but was otherwise used for museum storage. Eventually, the Grand Rapids Public Museum High School opened in 2018, breathing new life and energy into the vacant building.

Another historically significant building located just south of the museum is the Calkins Law Office. It is the oldest surviving structure in Grand Rapids and a perfect example of the Classical Revival architecture popular in the early nineteenth century. When it was built by the Kent Improvement Company in 1836, it was one of only thirteen frame buildings in the entire town. It was initially located on what is now the corner of Ottawa and Monroe. Pioneer Charles Philo Calkins used the three-room structure as his law office when he moved to Grand Rapids. He was born in Vermont and studied law, like his father. Calkins was admitted to the

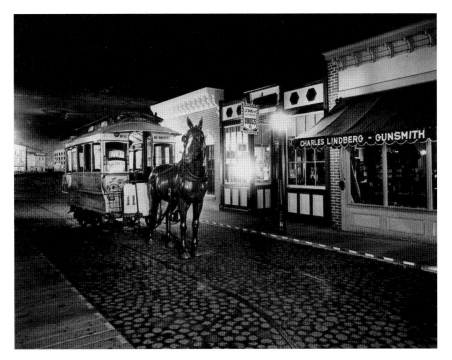

A glimpse of the former Gaslight Village. *Courtesy of the Grand Rapids Public Museum Collection.*

bar in 1836 and settled down in Grand Rapids, where he married Mary Hinsdale in 1839. He practiced in the building until around 1850, when he needed a larger space. In addition to being a lawyer and fathering eight children, Calkins served as the city's recorder, court solicitor and justice of the peace. He retired in 1880 and passed away ten years later at the age of eighty-seven.

The building was eventually moved to Ionia Street, where it was used as a private residence for many years. As it began to fall into disrepair, talk began of tearing it down. A local builder and active preservationist named John Stiles bought the structure in 1969 for $650, with the agreement that the building would be moved off the land within a reasonable amount of time. Stiles offered it to the city with the stipulation that it be located on the site of the old city hall clock tower. The city turned down the offer, saying that the move "would violate the spirit of urban renewal between parties in the project area."

With the help of others, Stiles continued to work on the building while looking for a new location. The home received new cedar roof shingles, paint and windows. Rotten molding was pulled out and replaced by specially made pieces. The fake brick siding that had been attached to the original pine planks was also removed. Finally, in 1971, the city agreed to accept the gift and place the building across the street from the museum in Lincoln Place Park on State and Washington Streets. The land itself had been deeded to the city in 1849 by a man named Canton Smith, an early settler. It was known as State Street Park until 1912, when philanthropist Loraine Pratt Immen came up with the idea of replacing the Civil War monument and fountain that is located downtown. She thought a full-length statue of Abraham Lincoln would be more appropriate. Her original idea was not endorsed, but she still commissioned a fifty-inch-tall bust of Lincoln that was eventually displayed in the newly named Lincoln Place Park. Once the Calkins Law Office was moved to its new location, many people helped bring it back to its former glory, including two young men from Boy Scout Troop 338, Travis Lepsch and Corey Alberda. A display outside the building lists many of the sponsors involved.

The Haunting

When I am asked if I have ever seen an actual ghost, I immediately think of the old Grand Rapids Public Museum. Although I grew up in a haunted house, all the strange figures I had seen there were shadowy and almost see-through. The first time I saw a spirit and honestly thought it was a living, breathing person was in the Gaslight Village.

Around 1989, my neighborhood friend Stacy Kolenda and I thought we were all grown up. Being around thirteen years old, we yearned for the feeling of independence and fulfilled that desire with day trips downtown. We didn't want to shop for clothes or look for boys like typical girls our age; we wanted to go to the museum. We would plan outings, days in advance, to take the bus and spend hours walking the halls. Stacy loved animals, so we would spend hours at the dioramas, then I would want to hang out in Gaslight Village, as I have always felt like I belong back in the old days. We'd end our trip with lunch at Big Boy on Pearl Street and a stop at Joe Vrana & Sons Tack Room, where we'd both enjoy the smell of fresh leather as Stacy shopped for horse gear. All these trips left me with amazing memories. There was one Tuesday morning trip during summer vacation, however, when things didn't go as planned.

The night before Stacy and I were supposed to leave, she called and said she had been grounded and couldn't go. I remember being crushed; then my crafty mind started to develop plan B. Knowing there was no way my parents would let me go downtown alone, I decided to play it off like Stacy was still going. They were both at work when I left by myself for the bus, with only a book for company. I got to the museum right after it opened and spent hours looking at only the things I wanted to. Life was good as I walked into Gaslight Village and decided to take a minute to rest my feet. I sat on a bench outside of the printer shop and took out my paperback. It was quiet and dark, too dark to read. Instead, I leaned back and took in my surroundings, thinking about how different things must have been in the past—harder but better, if you ask me. I heard a door close and watched as a woman, wearing a red Victorian dress that looked like it was made of velvet, walked out of the drugstore. Her hands were in a fluffy white muffler, and she looked like she came straight off a Christmas card. I assumed she was some reenactor working at the museum, as she looked completely solid. We made eye contact as she walked toward me. Once in front of the barbershop, she stopped. I let out a friendly hello. She tipped her head and smiled from ear to ear, then turned and walked through the door of the barbershop—not through the doorway, but through the door! I watched as she literally vanished in front of my eyes. It was at that point that I realized one thing. When you walked down the wooden sidewalk in Gaslight Village, you heard every step you took. Not once did I hear a footstep as she walked in my direction. I immediately got up and hightailed it out of there, running toward the planetarium. I vividly remember being so scared that when I left soon after, I used the exit doors on Washington Street. There was no way you could have gotten me to walk back alone through Gaslight Village that day.

Since I have begun to share my story, I have heard many accounts of spooky activity in the museum, several about a woman in red. In 2021, I met a woman named Amy who told me her teenage daughter Emily (name changed for privacy) was enrolled at the Public Museum High School. Emily told her mom all the time that the place has spirits. "My entire family is sensitive to the paranormal and has been for generations. My grandmother was well-known for being able to channel spirits directly. We're not that good," Amy said with a laugh, "but we both still see and hear things most people don't." Emily had told her mom about seeing the woman in red throughout the building on a few occasions. (As far as I know, I'm the only one who's ever seen the white muffler.) The first time,

The lady in red who has been seen in the old museum. *Roger Scholz*.

she saw what appeared to be a vortex forming at the bottom of the steps in the main lobby. Emily looked at her classmates but could tell that no one around her could see what was happening right in front of them. Slowly, a form took shape and began to ascend the stairs. By the time it reached the top of the stairs, Emily could see the figure was wearing a red dress. She said there was nothing malignant about the woman; it was almost like she was lost in time. She again saw the woman walking around a couple other times in the mezzanine area.

The primary reason Amy wanted me to change her daughter's name is the next story. She joked about having me print her daughter's full name in bold letters but said she'd rather stay on good terms with her. One day, Emily came home completely worked up and rushed into the bathroom. Once out, she told her mom that she had to go all day but was too embarrassed to do it at school. Early in the afternoon, she had to excuse herself and ran to the nearest restroom. Completely paranoid about "going" in front of anyone, she checked to see that all the stalls in the bathroom were empty, going so far as to push the doors open. Then she quickly sat down on the last toilet seat and let out what she called "the world's biggest fart." The bathroom door had not opened; no one had come in or gone out. Yet she heard a woman giggle and say, "Oh my!" Emily sat on the toilet, mortified. She said, "Excuse me," wiped and quickly washed her hands. On her way out, she again took note that no one was in the room with her. As she opened the door and started to walk out, she heard a woman say, "Happens to the best of us, love!"

I learned about the second specter quite by accident in 2015. I had been volunteering at the Grand Rapids City Archives on Washington Street, whose entrance is in the rear of the old museum. I had spent the morning scanning old photographs into their system, and my stomach was telling me it was time for a break. It was a beautiful sunny spring day, so I purchased a six-inch sub and picked a small grassy spot behind the museum to eat. It was close to the sidewalk but far enough back that I could spread out a little. I had a folder of articles with me that I was reading, jotting down notes on any interesting history I could share on my tour.

When my sandwich was half gone, I noticed a woman walking toward me with a beagle on a leash. Knowing I was within reach, I picked up my lunch to keep it away from the dog. As they got closer, the beagle walked over, smelled me, took three steps away and began to poop. The poor woman was mortified! Dying of embarrassment, she immediately began to apologize. I laughed and told her not to worry about it. I had kids and animals back at home and knew all about being embarrassed by them. She said, "You are the sweetest! What are all the papers? Are you doing research?" I introduced myself and explained to her that I was going to be doing a ghost tour and was researching facts on buildings in the area. Her eyes grew big, and she said, "Do you believe in fate? I have a story for you right here! I'm Rebecka, by the way!" She reached out to shake my hand and then pointed up at the back of the museum. "Do you see those three windows?" I nodded as she proceeded to tell me her story.

"Do you see the window on the far left? That is where I see him! Can I have your pencil?" Rebecka asked. At this point, she grabbed my white napkin and began to draw a picture of the man she has seen on countless occasions. "I take my dog Bow for a walk every evening when I get home from work. About six months ago, I started to see a man standing in that exact window looking down at me." She turned the napkin around and said, "I suck at drawing, but this gives you a rough idea." I looked at the faint pencil sketch she drew. The face that looked back was disfigured. While the head shape was normal, one side of his face seemed to sit lower than the other, appearing distorted, if not damaged.

"Who is he?" I asked. Rebecka shrugged her shoulders and went on with her story.

The back of the museum, where the spirit of a man has been spotted standing in the far left window. *Brad Donaldson.*

A drawing of the distorted man, based on the original napkin sketch. *Roger Scholz.*

"I would see him almost every night that I walked Bow. He would be standing looking out the window. I smiled at him, but he didn't seem to notice. After seeing him looking sad one day, I waved to him. I saw him smile and wave back. After that, I would see him maybe twice a week; each time I would wave, and he'd wave back. I felt good! It made me happy for him to know I cared. Then I had a visit."

At this point in the conversation, Rebecka seemed to get nervous. "I finished my walk and went back to my house. When you walk in, you are in the living room. A small kitchen is around the corner to the right. So I walk in, turn on the lights, hang up Bow's leash and go in the kitchen to fill up his water dish. As I set it down, Bow timidly comes walking around the corner, whimpering. I look at him and notice right away that his ears are down, and his tail is tucked between his legs. I instantly thought, *Someone is in the apartment*, so I grab a knife out of the butcher block, raise it and slowly walk into the living room. Sitting on the couch, I see this guy! Same face, sitting there looking at me! I could see his upper body, but I could see the couch cushion where his lower half should be!"

"Oh my God! What did you do?" I asked.

She said, "I quickly took two steps back into the kitchen, closed my eyes and said, 'Thanks for coming to visit, but you have to go now!'"

I honestly think I smirked as I thought, *That's a silly response.* I asked her what happened after that.

"Bow walked out into the living room and came running back into the kitchen straight for his water bowl. He was acting normal, so I looked around the corner, and the guy was gone!" She went on to say she hadn't seen him for weeks after that but recently noticed him in the window again. "I still smile and wave but tell him to stay where he is."

That day, I went back into the archives and scanned a bit longer before heading out to pick up my boys from school. I brought them home, made dinner, cleaned the kitchen and went upstairs to take a shower. Once out, I put on my bathrobe and opened the bathroom door to let out some steam, as we didn't have a fan. As I reached for a Q-tip, I glanced in the mirror that

The oldest structure in Grand Rapids, the Charles P. Calkins Law Office. *Brad Donaldson.*

was foggy on the bottom but clear on top. Standing in the hallway behind me was the exact same man that Rebecka had told me about. He was a little shorter than I expected; I would guess five feet, seven inches. His face looked exactly as she drew him: one eye looking at me and the other resting on his cheek, looking down at the floor. So what did I do? I closed my eyes tight and said, "Thanks for coming to visit, but you have to leave now!" When I opened my eyes, he was gone. I have never seen him at the museum, despite visiting that back window time and time again.

Numerous people have asked me if I know who the mysterious man is. While I have never found anyone matching his description, there is another reason I call the area Dead Man's Row. Between the years 1910 and 1920, there were thirteen different morticians located on this same small stretch of road. Many people who died in Grand Rapids filtered through this area at that time; maybe one stuck around.

The following year, I was telling a tour group about the lady in red and the man in the window when a pedestrian stopped to listen. After my spiel, she came up to me and said she had a similar story about a man in a window, but this time, it was at the Calkins Law Office. My interest piqued, I gave her a business card and received a call from her the next day. Her name is Samantha, and she told me about an experience she had.

The stately ghost of Charles P. Calkins. *Roger Scholz.*

I do my best to walk at least ten thousand steps a day, but after work, I was only a little over seven thousand. It was January and got dark early, but I figured there was still time to get my steps in. So I put on my boots, bundled up and hit the road! I had walked half an hour when it started to get dark, so I headed back toward my house. As I passed the Calkins building, I noticed a light was on, which was unusual because it's normally dark at night. Out of curiosity, I started to walk up the path to the door and noticed no footsteps in the fresh snow. I went up to the window on the right and saw a man sitting at a desk with what looked like an oil lamp. He was writing in a book. I figured he worked with the museum and was about to walk away when he glanced up at me. I noticed at that time that he had piercing blue eyes. He was an older guy, white hair, big beard—a grandpa type. Feeling out of place, I smiled and waved goodbye. I carefully went down the front steps, so I didn't slip, and headed back down the same path. I glanced up at the window again and noticed the light was out. Curiosity got the best of me, and I went back up to look in the window again. The man, the desk, the lamp: all of it was gone. I had never heard of ghost furniture! But I am 100 percent convinced I saw Charles Calkins! And I'm also convinced he's still wondering who the weird lady was looking in his office window.

When looking further into Calkins's life, I came across a description of him. It described Charles as having "blue eyes, deep and expressive gray whiskers and hair." I also discovered he was a Democrat. Could he be haunting the location because he has a bust of Abraham Lincoln, the first Republican president, on his front lawn staring down his office? It seems we all do crazy things when politics get brought up. The spirits seen in the area all seem to be friendly and a little bit curious. Perhaps they are just wondering why this stretch of road is so creepy.

CHAPTER 8

PIKE'S PEAK

LOCATION: 230 EAST FULTON STREET

Port Sheldon is a city that lies thirty-two miles to the west of Grand Rapids. It was first envisioned by a group of Pennsylvania financiers in the 1830s. They saw the land situated by Pigeon Lake and, imagining the waterway was deep enough to bring ships in, immediately thought it would be the investment of a lifetime. They hoped it would become a booming city like Chicago. They created the Port Sheldon Land Company and purchased six hundred acres of land for $900, with the intention of building a thriving city.

It started off successfully enough. Plans were laid out to construct prefabricated homes on 142 blocks, with twenty-four homes on each block. The city opened its first post office in 1838, followed by a general store, a church, a tavern, a lighthouse, a sawmill, a pier and two miles of railroad. The crown jewel of the town was the elaborate twenty-nine-room Ottawa House hotel, with six Greek columns adorning the front entrance. It alone cost $40,000 to build. Over $2 million was pumped into this project, which included the first road from Holland to Grand Haven, with Port Sheldon at the midpoint.

One of the men who worked with the company was Abram Ward Pike. He was born on a modest farm in Cincinnati, Ohio, on October 5, 1814—the second oldest of twelve children. He was a small, scrappy kid who quickly became known for his trapping skills. He first came to Michigan when he was thirteen to be an assistant at the Indian Mission School in the town of Niles. There, Abram learned the customs and languages of the Native

Young Abram Pike. *Courtesy of the Grand Rapids Public Library Historical Collection.*

people in the area. By the age of sixteen, he was fluent in several different Indian dialects, and he did all he could to help the local tribes, often acting as an interpreter for the government. He didn't think twice about calling out dishonest traders trying to take advantage of the Natives, becoming not only their protector but also their friend.

In 1833, Abram moved to St. Joseph and continued to make a name for himself as a fur trader, often traveling to trading posts in Chicago. He gained a reputation for being courageous and getting the job done. Several times he was called on to help visitors unfamiliar with the area travel throughout West Michigan, a land filled with wild animals, thick forests and few roads. The most famous of his adventures happened in the winter of 1842, what is known as "the hard winter" in all of Michigan's history books. By mid-November, well over two feet of snow had accumulated, and it stayed at least that deep through April. Documented temperatures for this storm reached twenty-two degrees below zero Fahrenheit. In December, a ship was sailing in Lake Michigan when a horrible snowstorm hit. It pushed the boat to the shores of Grand Haven, where it wrecked. Cold, tired and wearing iced-over clothes, the party of nine sailors and a cook set out to find their way to Grand Rapids. There, they could catch a stagecoach to Battle Creek and head home to Ohio. They hired Abram—whose reputation preceded him—to lead the party on the thirty-four-mile walk.

Abram brought along a local tribe member that he was close with, as well as Charles W. Hathaway (a sixteen-year-old boy). They hadn't gone far before they found themselves trudging through snowbanks up to their chins. The men took turns leading the group—throwing themselves into the snow to knock it down—as the rest walked single file behind. At the rear was Abram's favorite pony, known for being as white as snow. The drifts were so high that the group only covered about half a mile an hour. Late on the second day, the sailors began to lose faith in Abram, suspecting he was lost. Once the food ran out, they straight-up accused him of plotting with the Indians to lead them to the middle of nowhere, rob and kill them. Seeing the sailors panic, Abram immediately took charge. He knew they were close to their destination, yet the sailors were talking about turning back (a trip Abram knew they would not survive). For their own good, he instructed Charles and his Indian friend to remain in the back of the group with guns the pony had been carrying in a saddlebag. He instructed his friends to shoot any of the sailors if they got out of line and continued to force them to take turns as the leader. On the morning of the third day, they found two farmers from Grandville using a yoke of oxen to break a road through the snow. The rest of their trip went quickly. Abram's reputation as fearless but strict remained intact. Life was going well for him. He was working at a Native American trading post when he was offered the position of clerk and postmaster for the Port Sheldon Land Company. He also married a young lady named Elenora Louise Prior in 1841 and started a family.

Several different factors contributed to the demise of Port Sheldon. The unreliable banking system and the Panic of 1837 took their toll, but the final nail in the coffin was the sandbars. The investors discovered that the opening into Lake Pigeon was incredibly shallow, making it impossible for ships to pass through; no waterway meant no shipping. Supplies were short, and sickness set upon the town. A man named Hoyt Post from Vermont wrote about his stay at the Ottawa Hotel during this time. He described the front of the hotel as superb and decorated in "the most graceful manner." During dinner, he took note that everyone at the tables around him did nothing but complain about how bad conditions in the town had become. Despite his posh surroundings, Hoyt described getting a miserable night's sleep, during which he woke up freezing cold with a throbbing headache and a raging fever. A copy of the official register from the hotel showed only 112 guests lodged there between 1838 and 1843, 15 of whom were residents of Port Sheldon.

By 1844, the company had fallen into financial ruin, and the remaining three hundred occupants, mostly employees of the company, abandoned the city. Abram was given $500 to remain and liquidate the company's assets, as well as full access to the two-hundred-acre farm. He took his wife and two servants and moved into the hotel. Together, they raised one hundred acres of wheat that year, saving the money for their upcoming relocation. The town's furniture was peddled to Chicago for $5,000, and much of the lumber was sold to the City of Holland. In all, Abram was only able to sell off the hotel and thirty lots. The money raised wasn't even enough to pay for the paint and glass used in constructing the hotel. Once the town was dismantled, Abram relocated to Grand River Valley (what

Abram Pike's homestead on Fulton Street. *Brad Donaldson.*

we know now as Grand Rapids). He had first been to the area when he was thirteen, arriving on Christmas Day, and its natural beauty had made a lasting impression on him.

Abram chose to build his home on the outskirts of the village on what would come to be known as Fulton Street. The residence was rumored to be modeled after the United States Bank at Philadelphia. A most impressive achievement is that Abram dragged four of the massive Greek columns from the defunct Ottawa House hotel in Port Sheldon through the thick woods by oxcart to use in his new home. He also brought smaller columns from the train depot, which he used to flank the side porches. He was upcycling before any of us. When the home was completed in 1845, it was surrounded by woods. Grand Rapids didn't become an official city for five more years.

Once established in town, Abram worked with Colonel Amos Roberts & Son's store, located in an old red warehouse on Waterloo (now known as Market Avenue). Twice a year, the local tribes of Ottawa (Odawa), Chippewa (Ojibwa) and Potawatomi Indians received payments from the government. When that compensation was handed out, they were asked to enter through the door on the riverside and exit through the door on Market Avenue. To leave, they had to walk past the vendors that had extended them credit all year, some of whom hadn't yet received payment. Abram, however, never had an issue getting paid. When he was ninety-one, he stated that while he annually sold thousands of dollars' worth of goods on credit to the tribes over the years, he only lost about one hundred dollars total on bad accounts.

During his lifetime, Abram held several different titles of importance: constable in 1850, marshal in 1851 and city assessor in 1852, just to name a few. In 1858, he was part of the group that helped build a new lattice bridge over the Grand, the only bridge in the area to cross the river at that time. (This bridge sat where Michigan and Bridge Street currently meet.) After his wife, Elenora, passed in 1853, he married Miss Eliza J. Roberts in 1855. In total, Abram had seven children (two boys and five girls).

While photos of Abram as an older man give the impression that he was stern and a bit grumpy, he was known to be a kind man. He had a soft spot for animals, particularly his white pony that accompanied him on his many journeys. With Abram's care, the pony lived to be well over forty years old, spending the last half of its life in luxury, grazing on the estate. Abram also did all he could for his friends, including the local Native Americans. When the weather turned cold, he would generously let as many as forty men, women and children stay in his warm and roomy basement.

Abram passed away in his home of arteriosclerosis and a dilated heart on October 15, 1906, at the age of ninety-three. As was traditional at the time, his funeral took place in the house. The family continued to live there until 1920, when Abram's daughter deeded the property to the Grand Rapids Art Gallery. (The city's first building that housed art had been destroyed in 1919 by a fire, along with $100,000 in artwork.) Emily Clark, a local socialite and philanthropist, donated $50,000 to fund the project, which opened in 1924. She had accumulated an extensive collection of paintings in her home, known as the Paddock Place, at 1033 Lake Drive SE (some may also remember it as Gibson's or Mangiamo Italian Restaurant!). Emily's paintings were donated to the art museum, making up most of its original exhibits. A fireproof brick gallery was added behind the Pike home in 1928, and additional galleries were added in 1930. Over the years, significant damage from Michigan's weather and old age took a toll on the home. The Grand Rapids Art Museum had also outgrown the space, so it moved to the former Federal Building. Design Quest Furniture Company took over, making improvements while using the location for their business. It was sold again in 1990 to J.T. French Co., a different design and furniture business.

New life was breathed into Pike House when Design Plus discovered it. The company first opened its doors in 1979 at a small location in downtown Grand Rapids and soon found itself in need of a larger place. It purchased

Right: The grave site of Abram Pike. *Brad Donaldson.*

Below: The front parlor of Pike House. *Brad Donaldson.*

the freight depot on the corner of Cherry Street and Ionia Avenue, which was originally built in 1905. Design Plus was proud to revitalize the building and preserve a piece of history at the same time. When the company became aware of the deteriorating Pike House in 2006, it again stepped up to the plate. A year was spent identifying original details, such as wall colors, trim and crown moldings. Design Plus restored the building to its former glory, leaving the original living room as the reception area.

The most recent owners, the law firm of Keller & Almassian, acquired the building in 2013. They were looking for a downtown location where they could set up individual lawyers with complementary, not competing, practices. As soon as lawyer A. Todd Almassian stepped into the building, he knew it was something special, and he did all he could to push the sale along. A huge history buff, he began to dig into the past and collect all he could find about Abram Pike, Port Sheldon and the home.

During the 2014 renovations, the doors were closed, and fences surrounded the building. Imagine the owners' surprise when a woman named Anita Gilleo suddenly appeared inside the home and introduced herself as the granddaughter of famed impressionist painter Mathias Alten. Mathias, a Grand Rapids resident, is known as one of the greatest impressionist painters of his time. He was born in Germany in 1871 and immigrated to Michigan with his parents, settling down on the west side of Grand Rapids. Later in life, Alten traveled to Europe, where he

These horseshoes are just a couple of the items on display that were found on the grounds. *Brad Donaldson.*

painted landscapes and portraits with the masters. By the time he passed away in 1938, he had made quite a name for himself in the art world. His granddaughter informed the lawyers that in his teen years, Alten had been hired to paint signs around town, including one at the art gallery. Immediately, workers looked and found "The Grand Rapids Art Gallery" carved into the façade under some easy-to-remove boards. (It was updated years later when the name changed to "Museum.") Even bits of original gold leaf were visible on the sign. Considering it a historical treasure, the owners had the sign taken down and moved inside to preserve it from further weather damage.

Todd Almassian proudly exhibits historical items of significance throughout the office. In one of the boardrooms, the original floor plans from the home are framed and hanging on the wall—the same floor plans that have been filed with the Library of Congress as the first example of early Greek Revival architecture in Grand Rapids. In the back hallway, there is a shelf displaying items that were dug up on the property over the years, particularly in the area that is now the parking lot. This includes jars, bottles and two rusted horseshoes that Almassian believes could have belonged to Abram's prized white pony.

The Haunting

One day in the 1990s, I walked into a small art shop that was located on Fulton Street called Douma's Art Supplies. While looking for a smudge stick for my pencil drawings, I had no choice but to eavesdrop on a conversation the owner was having with a woman across the room. They were discussing how maintenance and upkeep of old downtown buildings was so expensive. "You fix one thing at Pike House, and another breaks," she said with a laugh. Clueless about what the Pike House was, I asked her its location. "Two doors down, big white pillars," she said with a smile. Immediately, I knew the home she was talking about. I remembered driving by it as a child and telling my mom I wanted to live there one day because it looked like a miniature version of the White House. Instantly, my tag line came out of my mouth: "Ever have anything weird or unexplainable happen there?" She gave me the quizzical look I get a lot but then responded, "I have." I never officially got her name but always remembered her stories. I've always referred to her as Dee (for Douma's).

Back hallway, where the ghost of Abram Pike has been spotted. *Brad Donaldson.*

From the first moment she walked into Pike House, Dee felt like something was watching her—not in a bad, creepy way but more of a welcoming "Do you need anything?" kind of way. She always chalked it up to her imagination until, as she put it, "the folder thing happened." Dee had been working on a project for a client and accidentally misplaced their file. She'd had it earlier in the day and retraced her steps but wasn't able to find it. After searching for over an hour, Dee fell back into her chair, defeated, and closed her eyes. She sighed, opened her eyes and looked up. That's when she saw the missing folder sitting on the desk, as clear as day. Seconds earlier, the table had been empty! I asked her if she thought a spirit was messing with her, but Dee thought just the opposite. She explained that earlier in the day, she had put away tons of folders and believed she may have accidentally filed this one in the wrong spot; the spirit was kind enough to help her out. She considered it a sweet gesture and said, "Thanks for helping" loudly to her invisible friend.

The next encounter Dee had was a little more intense. Walking down the hallway toward the back of the building, she rounded the corner and came face to face with a gentleman. She described him as average height and around forty years old. He was dressed in what she assumed they would have worn in the olden days. When I asked her if anything stood out about him, she said, "His facial hair. He had a beard and no moustache— you never see that anymore!" Was she afraid? Not one bit. She explained that the man was too polite to be scary. As soon as they saw each other, he smiled at her, tipped his hat and bent at the waist. He then turned toward the water fountain, took about seven or eight invisible steps upward and disappeared. Up until that point, he had looked as real as you and I. Although she wasn't sure of the year, Dee said she remembered this took place in October because when she told her friends what she had seen, they all giggled at her and said, "Of course you saw a ghost in October! Was it a Halloween decoration?"

I first reached out to Keller & Almassian in 2015 as I was putting together a new tour route. I wanted to add Pike House as a stop but wouldn't do it without their permission. (Especially in this case; no one wants a group of angry attorneys coming after them!) I made an appointment with Todd Almassian, as I had heard he was the expert on the home's history. I know from experience that a lot of professionals laugh and roll their eyes when I tell them what I do on the side. This was not the case with Todd. A true gentleman, he shook my hand and asked what he could do to help. He gave me a tour of the entire building, including the gallery in back and the empty brick basement that formerly housed the Native Americans. When I asked him if he had ever experienced anything unexplainable, he said he hadn't. Although he didn't come out and say he doesn't believe in ghosts, I got the impression he's a "I'll believe it when I see it, and even then, I'll question it" kind of guy. I told him about the sighting Dee had of the man with a beard and no moustache. Almassian immediately told me to follow him. We walked into a conference room, where he pointed to a picture of Abram Pike, a man I had never seen before. In it, Abram looked stoically to the side, sporting a beard with no moustache. Coincidence?

After one of my tours in 2021, a sweet lady named Sue came up to talk to me. She worked at the art museum in the 1970s and truly believed the building was haunted. She often heard heavy footfalls throughout the home when no visitors were there. When I asked her who she thought it was, she immediately replied, "It's a man's energy. Maybe Mr. Pike is still running the show over there." Sue spoke of hearing men's voices chatting and laughing in other areas of the building, particularly when there was an exhibition on tribal culture going on.

"I would hear two or three voices in the next room, but when I went in, the chattering would move to another room. I could never pin them down." The other event Sue mentioned was hearing a man's sigh come from the small west room in the front of the house. I shared with her that during the initial walkthrough given to me in 2015, Todd Almassian spoke of hearing that Abram had passed away in that same room. (While we do know that Abram died in the home, neither of us was able to find any documentation saying it was in that room.)

The courteous spirit of Abram Pike. *Roger Scholz.*

I went back to visit Keller & Almassian again in September 2023. What a difference eight years make! The giant gallery that stood in the back now holds offices that are faithful to the originality of the home's past. The murky, musty basement has been replaced by new workspaces with stunning original details like river rock walls and hand-hewn wooden beams with axe marks. Todd Almassian has also left a mark of his own on the home for future owners to talk about. During renovations, the old basement carpet was pulled up, and new concrete had to be put down. A decision was made to diamond polish the concrete, but before doing that, Todd pushed Petoskey stones his children had found down in the drying floor. (Petoskey stones are rocks with fossils unique to the Great Lakes that surround the state of Michigan.) This left a beautiful touch of his own for future generations to enjoy. While Todd credits Design Plus for their work on the restoration, I hope he realizes that like Abram Pike, he and his firm have had an equal impact on the property. In one hundred years, in addition to talking about Abram, citizens of Grand Rapids will be talking about the law firm that took

Old Abram Pike. *Courtesy of the Grand Rapids Public Library Historical Collection.*

on the role of preserving the history of Abram's home and saw to it that Abram Pike got the recognition he deserved as a pioneer of this city.

When Judith Baxter, attorney at law, was younger, her mother would drop her off every Saturday when this building was the old art museum. "I would come in through the back and go into the studio downstairs and get into all kinds of things. One time, I remember making a clay lion that was so good the art director wanted to buy it, but my dad wouldn't sell it to him." She still has her lion to this day, a reminder of the good times when life was much simpler. "To this day, when I walk in the building, I can still smell oil paint and clay. It makes me smile."

I also had the pleasure of meeting paralegal Nicole Zuidema. She admits to spending lots of time in the home but has never picked up on anything out of the ordinary. She loves working in the building, especially in December when she can crank up the holiday music and get the decorations out for Christmas. One particular year, there seemed to be an electrical issue. She joked out loud, "Okay, Mr. Pike, knock it off! I'm just making your house look pretty." I myself got a chuckle out of this because when I first saw the older photo of Abram Pike, it reminded me of sketches I have seen of Ebenezer Scrooge.

The last thing Nicole shared with me was regarding the supposed "room of death." After I told her about the man's gasp that had been heard and the rumor about Abram dying there, she got the heebie-jeebies. She shared that out of the entire place, there was one attorney who worked there who purposely avoided using that room. "She would say it had a bad energy." I have been to a ridiculous number of haunted locations. Being sensitive, I've walked into places where the energy is so negative, I have burst into tears. The energy at the Pike House is nothing but friendly. If there is a ghost remaining in this home, I do believe it is Abram Pike. I don't think he's there to haunt those in his home, just to keep a watchful eye over his new "family" that has moved in.

CHAPTER **9**

THIS SIDE OR THAT

LOCATION: MONROE CENTER STREET AND SHELDON AVENUE NE

One thing that can be said about Mortimer Perrin is that he was a
hard worker. Even though it was summer and most fourteen-year-
olds were in bed sleeping at five forty-five on a Tuesday morning,
Mortimer had already gotten up, washed, dressed, eaten and was walking
to his job. His parents had brought them to Grand Rapids from Brooklyn,
New York, to be closer to family who lived in Lowell. They had arrived only
three months prior and taken up residence in a small apartment located at 99
South Division. His father, William, was a carriage driver for the Columbian
Transfer Company, while his mother, Addie, stayed home to care for his
three-year-old brother, Lester. Mortimer wanted to do all he could to help his
family and was elated when a local dentist hired him to help around the office.

Dr. Edward C. Vietor was best known for fixing teeth with dental bridges,
instead of using plates like many dentists at that time. He ran a successful
practice on the second floor of the Kendall Building, which stood facing
Monument Park on Monroe Center. The structure itself was built in the
early 1880s and named after George Kendall, a Grand Rapids businessman
who came to the area in 1846 and made his fortune in the grocery and dry
goods trade. To this day, the building stands out as unique, having been
constructed of redbrick and sandstone.

It was July 22, 1902. Having been employed by the doctor for only two
months, Mortimer wanted to show his gratitude by surprising the dentist with

The Kendall Building where Mortimer fell twenty feet, resulting in his death. *Brad Donaldson.*

freshly cleaned windows when he came to work that morning. He let himself into the building and filled a bucket with soap and water. Mortimer expertly washed the inside of the three windows and, grabbing his cleaning supplies, stepped out onto the ledge that stood over the Jarvis Bicycle & Sporting Goods Company. One by one, he began to wash the outside windows. The first two went smoothly, but on the third, he went to throw a cup of dirty water over the edge and lost his balance. A man named Huntley Russell was passing below at the time, and the boy's body brushed against him as he fell to the hard stone ground below. Narrowly avoiding injury himself, Huntley watched as Mortimer landed on the right temple of his skull with his arm bent underneath him.

Thinking he was dead, Huntley quickly rushed Mortimer into the bicycle shop. They could see that his temple was crushed and his right wrist was fractured. Three doctors with a practice nearby (Luton, Campbell and Griswold) rushed over to help. At first, they agreed the injuries were fatal and there was no reason to move the teen to a hospital. But after a few minutes, Mortimer began to stir. His respiration and pulse grew stronger, so they rushed him by police ambulance to the Union Benevolent Association (UBA) Hospital on College Avenue.

Mortimer's skull fracture extended from the top of his head down to his nose, causing him to bleed excessively. The hospital's medical team injected him with a salt solution to slow the blood loss and hurried him into surgery. Although the surgical team relieved the pressure on his brain, Mortimer's life continued to slip away. After falling twenty feet shortly after eight o'clock in the morning, Mortimer Perrin was pronounced dead at 10:30 a.m. His body was brought to O'Brien Brothers Mortuary and eventually laid to rest at a family plot in Oakwood Cemetery in Lowell, Michigan.

An official inquest was held, but no one was found to be negligent, and Mortimer's death was ruled an accident. Four days later, the coroner's jury recommended an ordinance for the city of Grand Rapids that would require all building owners to place protective bars across the outside of their windows for the exclusive benefit of window cleaners. When one of the officials showed up at the city marshals' workplace to discuss how to go about enforcing the matter, he was all but laughed out of the office. According to the *Grand Rapids Press*, the city marshals "were treated to an amusing ten minutes" as the city official was shown there would not be room for the window cleaner to work between the window and the protective bars in one case out of a hundred, not to mention the "injury to the appearance of the building." The coroner's jury decided to let the matter drop.

Over the years, additional buildings sprouted up around the Kendall. Probably the most notable addition was made in 1916, when a triangular brick structure was added to the corner of Monroe Center and Sheldon Avenue. While all these buildings stood alone, they butted up against each other, giving the appearance of one long string of buildings that housed everything from dime stores to insurance—even an Arthur Murray Dance Studio. Being located by one of the busiest intersections downtown made it a popular location with lots of foot traffic. In August 1980, a fire broke out, leaving the corner structure unusable for several years. It was eventually purchased and donated to the Grand Rapids Children's Museum, which opened in 1997. It is hard to miss this building today, primarily due to the

The plot where Mortimer was laid to rest with family. *Brad Donaldson.*

hundred-foot-long bricolage mosaic that lines the east side. Known as *Imagine That!*, the mural created by Tracy Van Duinen took second place in Grand Rapids' popular ArtPrize competition in 2009.

The Haunting

I have spent my fair share of time at the Grand Rapids Children's Museum over the years. Personal visits with family, school outings and company events have brought me to this location countless times. When I would first walk in, I always sensed that someone unseen was there with us, but that feeling would soon be drowned out by the chaotic energy only a room full of children can bring.

The first time I pinned one of the employees down to ask if she thought the space was haunted, I was there with my nephew Josh in 1999. As he played with the bubbles, a young lady named Evelyn told me she had no doubts the place had a friendly visitor. No matter where she was in the building, she never felt alone. She would see movement out of the corner of her eye, like a small child running from room to room. "At first, I thought my eyes were going bad, but I would only see it when I was here. Later, I mentioned it to a couple of the people I work with, and they said they'd seen the same thing! We're convinced it's the ghost." Evelyn also shared that there were many times she would be upstairs cleaning, long after the last kid had left the building, and she would hear giggling and a child's footsteps running around downstairs.

During one of my son's school outings years later, I spoke to a teenage boy named Jack who had worked there for a couple months before he heard the place was supposedly haunted. Not being a believer in such things, Jack figured it was made up—that is, until the day he was working in the gift shop.

I remember it was on a Saturday in February because the weather was bad. We thought the place would be dead because the roads had a foot of snow…Wrong! The place was packed! At one point when everyone had left the gift shop, I saw what looked like a ball of light floating over the bookshelves in the front window. I had no clue what it was but watched as it flew into a book that was sitting back on a stand. The book then flipped forward onto the floor, and the ball of light disappeared. I thought it was weird but was already telling myself my eyes must be playing tricks on me. That is, until the book on the right of that one did the same thing, then the next one, then the next. I sat there and watched five different books that were leaning back on stands defy gravity and flip forward on their own. My initial reaction was to laugh. I have never believed in any religion or put much thought into the afterlife, but it was the first time I started to think— my God, there really must be something out there.

When I asked Jack if it scared him, he said he felt whoever or whatever it was seemed to be playful, not threatening.

On that same visit, a woman who was working at the front desk told me about how the basement is where a lot of the activity takes place. "You are never alone when you are in the basement!" she said with a chuckle. She went on to explain that because of the way the buildings are lined up next to each other, they have access doors to get into each other's basements— primarily used by utility workers such as plumbers or electricians.

Even though we are separated by being in different buildings, our basements connect with a door. For the door to open, both sides need to unlock their side, so it's not like we can barge into the building next door without their saying so. In fact, we rarely open the door. The weirdest thing is the store next to us will find items that belong here in the museum on their side of the locked door. They'll find blocks, balls and other items that literally "appear" on their side as if they've teleported there. It's crazy!

The last story I want to share is the one that means the most to me now, although it didn't at the time it took place in 2006. I had brought my two nephews, Brendan (seven) and Ethan (five), with me to the museum. At the time, I had no idea that a boy named Mortimer had even existed in Grand Rapids. We were on the main floor, and I was sitting by a window watching them play with another boy who was there. The three would play with the blocks, move to the next attraction, play with that for five minutes and then bounce on to the next. The one thing that caught my eye was that the other boy kept talking to his imaginary friend. At one point, the boy even held open a door for his friend to come through. I asked the lady next to me if it was her son, and she said, "Yes, that's Julius and his amazing imagination!" She went on to tell me that they came to the

The playful spirit of Mortimer. *Roger Scholz.*

museum at least once a week and that Julius had recently started talking to his pretend friend, not only at the museum but also at home. To this day, I get chills when I recall what she said next. "I've been trying to get him out of the house more. He loves watching TV. I think he even named his imaginary friend after a character in the Mickey Mouse Clubhouse—Mortimer." At the time, I had not yet learned about the sad death of a boy that took place only feet away.

While we all hope Mortimer Perrin has gone on to a better place, if you're a kid and must get "stuck" somewhere, the Grand Rapids Children's Museum would be a pretty cool place to spend eternity. With its train table, Legos and continually changing exhibits, perhaps Mortimer is enjoying making new friends now that he doesn't have to be up for work the next morning.

CHAPTER 10

I WILL WATCH YOUR CHILDREN

LOCATION: 227–233 EAST FULTON STREET

T here are two magnificent stone buildings that stand out on East Fulton Street: First United Methodist Church and the Masonic temple. While each has its own special history, there is one thing they have in common—the same ghost.

First United Methodist Church was the first established church in the Grand River Valley. It was formed in 1835 by a group of pioneers who were known as the Grand River Mission. In 1840, they purchased the southeast lot on the corner of Division and Fountain Streets and built a modest wooden church that became known as the Old White Church. As the congregation grew, the old church was replaced with a new building and pipe organ in 1869. This house of worship was humorously nicknamed the Church of the Holy Toothpicks because of the number of spires that adorned the rooftop.

Forty-seven years later, the congregation once again outgrew their building and so purchased a new plot of land on the corner of East Fulton and Barclay Streets. The church hired the popular architectural firm of Robinson & Campau. Both men, Frederick Robinson and Antoine B. Campau, were related to Louis Campau, the founding father of Grand Rapids who died in 1871. The new church cost approximately $212,000 to build and was dedicated in April 1916. The structure was built of limestone that was shipped from Sandusky, Ohio.

The very first Grand Rapids Masonic Temple Building was built in 1896 by E. Crofton Fox, a Thirty-Second Degree Mason. It was a seven-story

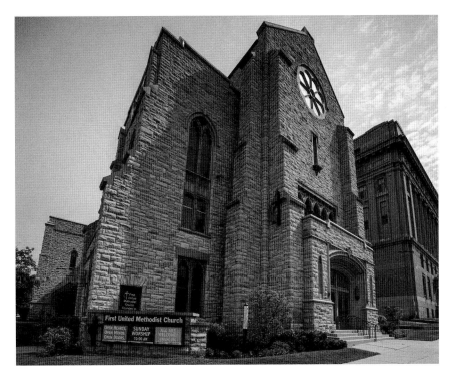

First United Methodist Church. *Brad Donaldson.*

building that sat on the corner of Louis Street and Ionia Avenue. As the order grew in popularity, grand and extravagant temples began to pop up around the United States. Grand Rapids was not a city to be left in the dust. The Masons formed a committee and raised enough funds for a new structure. The architectural father/son duo named Osgood & Osgood were hired. In 1912, land was purchased near the corner of Fulton Street and Lafayette Avenue from Edwin Sweet, a lawyer and former mayor of Grand Rapids from 1904 to 1906.

Construction on the new Masonic temple began on June 11, 1914. Things went smoothly for the first couple months, but that all changed shortly after eleven o'clock in the morning on Friday, November 13. A tremendous crash was heard throughout the entire business district as a large derrick used for lifting steel girders collapsed. A thirty-five-year-old man named Egbert Verhey was painting thirty feet in the air when the broken crane toppled down, striking the platform he was standing on. He was hurled into the basement with such force that his skull was fractured, four ribs were broken and the kneecap of one leg was shattered. After hours of excruciating pain,

Egbert died the following night. After only being in Grand Rapids for less than four days, he was interred at the Oakhill Cemetery.

Rumors instantly began to fly around the city that someone had tampered with the crane. At the time of the accident, there were two different factions of ironworkers on the site, which caused a bit of tension between the opposing organizations. After a thorough investigation, it was proven that a faulty clamp was responsible for the accident. Less than a month later, another terrible incident occurred around noon on Saturday, December 7. The workmen were on the verge of calling it a day but decided to hoist one last steel beam into place. As it was raised, a wooden derrick snapped, causing a huge mass of steel to plunge down, landing inches away from one man's face. Two others were not so lucky. H.W. Sobert was jarred from the structure and seriously wounded, and Harry Miller from Toledo was gravely injured.

Before construction was complete, even more accidents occurred. This included a man falling from the third floor, scaffolding that was holding eight

Grand Rapids Masonic Center. *Brad Donaldson.*

men collapsing underneath their feet and a man falling down the elevator shaft. One must wonder: was it bad luck, or was the project cursed? Whatever the answer, the building was soon completed. Its first big event was held on Friday, November 19, 1915. The Masonic fair was open to the public and was in full swing for eight days straight. There was something for everyone, from dancing to movies to food, candy and balloons.

The highlight of the first night was when President Woodrow Wilson turned on the new electric lights in the Grand Rapids building all the way from Washington, D.C. The Western Union Telegraph Company had connected phone wires at the U.S. capital to the electric control panel at the temple. At the stroke of seven o'clock in the evening, sitting in the Blue Room of the White House with several national officers of the Masonic fraternity, President Wilson flipped the switch—illuminating the inside of the temple, as well as six big searchlights outside (all focused on the façade).

The Haunting

One person who is known to haunt the Masonic temple is a gentleman named Lou Winsor. Brother Lou was active in Michigan and national Masonic work for over half a century, holding every state Masonic office at one time or another.

Brother Lou had a great passion for the work that he did and felt his fraternal brothers were family. He would spend countless hours working on projects in the temple before descending the center staircase of the building and walking outside. From there, he would enter a small underground tunnel under the east side of the building that led to a room designated as the Masons' smoking and card room. This Masonic "man cave" was one of Lou's favorite places to be. Brother Lou Winsor died on November 8, 1936, at the age of seventy-eight, from cerebral thrombosis (a blood clot in the brain) after being ill for ten days. Based on the countless sightings I have heard about, Brother Lou is what we call a residual spirit. He is like an imprint that was left on the environment; think video on replay. He does not interact with people and seems to take no notice of anyone around him. His ghost has only been seen wearing a blue suit, walking the same path he did in life—with his journey ending when he walks through the door at the end of the tunnel.

The ghost story that has been around the longest centers on First United Methodist Church. When I was collecting tales for my tour, I knew I had

The ghost of Brother Lou Winsor has been seen inside and out of the Masonic temple. *Roger Scholz.*

to stop by the church and inquire if it had any paranormal activity. Having been raised a practicing Catholic, I was a bit nervous about the reaction I would receive. The idea of walking into a house of worship to ask if it had a ghost left me feeling like I was about to receive a lecture. What I found was quite the opposite. I took a deep breath and walked into the church.

I quickly introduced myself to the receptionist and explained that I was putting together a ghost tour and would be bringing groups past the location. I asked if there was anything interesting about the history of the building that I could share—and casually threw in, "Or stories of anything odd or unexplainable." Without hesitation, she handed me contact information for two people. The first was I.J. Hiler, the church historian who cowrote the book *A History of First United Methodist Church, Grand Rapids, Michigan*. The second person was a woman named Molly who had been a member of the church for many years.

The church historian was kind enough to take me on a tour of the entire location, from basement to steeple. With her vast knowledge, it was obvious she knew the building inside and out. Along the way, she pointed out countless architectural highlights, such as the Italian terrazzo floors and the Tiffany window that stands fourteen feet high and twenty-six feet across.

Later that week, I also met up with Molly. She was quite welcoming. She guided me to the original ladies' parlor located behind the wall of the sanctuary, and our talk turned to the paranormal. Molly started her story: "While I was working in the church during the 1960s, we started a group of young adults who came together to meet other young people. They came to play games, talk and simply hang out. On one of those evenings, a person brought in a new board game, a Ouija board." I gasped at that point in her story, because I personally would never have brought something considered so negative into a church.

While this game has been around for hundreds of years, Parker Brothers officially released its version in 1966. When it first came out, it did not have negative connotations associated with it, like it does today. Some individuals can and do have positive experiences with Ouija. Still, most people in the paranormal field believe playing with one is a lot like leaving your front door open when you live in a bad neighborhood. A good soul could walk in, but so could a malicious one. Do you really want to take a chance?

Molly was there the night the young people decided to give the Ouija board a try. The game was set up on a table, and a young man and a young woman each put their hand on the planchette, which immediately started to move. When they asked who was talking, a name was spelled out: E-D-Y-T-H-E. When they asked "Edythe" why she was there, it spelled out that she had "lived close in the 1920s" and died of "Pulanski disease at a young age." When asked why she had not yet moved on, Edythe spelled out that she had stayed because she enjoyed the area when she was alive. As you can imagine, everyone was intrigued at the thought of talking to a ghost. One of

The original ladies' parlor where the Ouija board was used to contact Edythe. *Brad Donaldson.*

the young women who was there that night worked in the records room at Butterworth Hospital. (Keep in mind, this is before HIPAA laws went into effect.) She decided to do some digging on her own time to try and prove the existence of Edythe. She went through all the medical files but found no record of the name Edythe. What she did find was a Dr. Pulanski who had a medical practice in Grand Rapids during the 1930s. Could this doctor have diagnosed Edythe and named her disease after himself?

Several weeks had passed since the Ouija board was used, and people were still talking about it. Word got back to one of the pastors of the church. (This part always sounds like I am about to tell a bad bar joke.) This pastor had a friend who happened to be a rabbi, and during one of their early morning jogs, they talked about Edythe. The rabbi was intrigued. Soon after this, the rabbi invited the pastor and several friends to have dinner at his home. He asked the pastor to "Bring the board!" That evening, after dinner was finished and the rabbi's children had been put to bed, the group sat in the living room and placed the Ouija board on the coffee table. Hands were put on the planchette, and the questions began. "Is anyone here?" The board spelled out, "EDYTHE." The rabbi went on to ask, "Edythe, do you have a message for us?" The board spelled out, "I WILL WATCH YOUR CHILDREN." Immediately, the rabbi was concerned. He ran upstairs to check on his two boys. Both were sleeping soundly, and all was peaceful. Relieved, he went back downstairs, but he couldn't shake the feeling that something was wrong.

Several days later, early in the morning, the rabbi called the pastor and said, "Did you see the news this morning?" He went on to say that a man had been arrested close to his home as he was trying to abduct a child. The rabbi was convinced Edythe had stayed around to help keep his sons safe. Years later, in speaking about Edythe, the rabbi said he was convinced that Edythe had stayed in their home for several years. The entire family felt her presence, and they would smell roses when they talked about her. It was not until both boys graduated and moved out of the home that the rabbi stopped sensing her presence.

As I stood outside the parlor listening to Molly tell me this story, we both suddenly became aware of the scent of roses. No one had moved. No air fresheners were plugged in. The delightful aroma came out of nowhere and seemed to disappear just as quickly.

I have spent hours trying to determine who Edythe could have been when she was alive. With the few details that have been passed down, I have been able to narrow down the list. While I am not 100 percent convinced she is our suspect, I discovered a young lady named Edythe Mae Oster who lived on Ottawa Street. She perished on February 24, 1932, after a two-year battle with chronic intestinal nephritis. She was only seventeen years old when she died in her home.

Another woman named Edythe Cheer, who was a twenty-four-year-old housewife, died in 1926 from pulmonary tuberculosis at the city sanitarium located in downtown Grand Rapids. She seemed to be the best candidate, but then I discovered she lived in Jenison and grew up in Hudsonville. Would a ghost consider that "nearby"?

Whoever she is, Edythe continues to remain busy. One night on one of my tours, I discovered that I had several people in the group who had worked at the First United Methodist Church. Before we parted ways, they shared several experiences with me. One of the men had been standing alone in the back of the church when he heard a definitive "Hey!" whispered in his ear by a female voice. He looked around but could find no explanation for what he had heard. Then one of his friends shared another experience with me. He was helping to watch the children during a worship service, and there was a four-year-old boy who did not like being away from his parents. To calm the little boy, this man took him to the rear of the church, where the child could get a glimpse of his mom and dad. Once the boy saw his parents, he realized he had not been abandoned, and he calmed down. They walked back and forth in the narthex (an antechamber at the western entrance of the church). The man said, "We're in the back of the

The narthex where Edythe has been seen. *Brad Donaldson.*

church walking back and forth when I turn and see a woman standing on the other side of the area. She looked completely out of place—a long brown dress with tiny buttons down the front and hair pulled up tight. She looked over at me, smiled and nodded her head and then completely vanished before my eyes. I thought I was losing my mind, but then I heard the little boy who was with me say 'Cool!' He had seen her disappear too! That was a tough one to explain to his parents."

I also spoke with a young woman named Anna who was a ballerina in the Grand Rapids Ballet. She was in her early twenties and was super excited to share her story with me. First, she told me that she had seen Edythe—again in a brown dress, hair in a bun—but this time, at the Masonic temple. Anna told me that when she was around seventeen, the GR Ballet was having a photo shoot on the fourth floor. (At the time, the Grand Rapids Ballet was renting space in the basement to store costumes.)

We were in this large room that had a fainting couch set up for the photo shoot. It was me and about fifteen other teenage girls. We were all dressed like prim and proper ballerinas, but we weren't acting like it. We were running around acting crazy, doing jumps, and laughing…straight up being obnoxious. Suddenly, we all stopped at the same time and looked

110

toward the door. Standing there was a stern-looking woman giving us a dirty look. She raised her finger up to her lips and shushed us right before she vanished into thin air. Every one of us girls started screaming and ran out the door on the other side of the room. It took the photographer forever to finally get us calmed down enough to get the shots he came for that day.

The lighthearted spirit of Edythe.
Roger Scholz.

One night on my tour, as I was telling the ballerina story to the crowd, I noticed one man's eyes getting bigger and bigger with each detail I shared. As soon as I wrapped up my spiel, he came hurrying up to me. He always knew he had seen a ghost, but I had described exactly what he saw on the fourth floor of the Masonic temple. He explained that he was a contractor who worked lots of odd jobs on the site and has for years. He had seen the "brown lady" on three occasions—always looking in on him to see what he was up to before vanishing before his eyes.

The story of Edythe has become a spoken tradition at the church. Sometimes Edythe's legend is shared with the youth of the church (usually around Halloween). We will never know whether she found peace during her lifetime, but it seems she has found a loving home at First United Methodist Church during her afterlife.

CHAPTER 11

SWEET MEMORIES

LOCATION: 254 EAST FULTON STREET

O nly one term…" is what Martin L. Sweet told everyone when he was elected the first Republican mayor of Grand Rapids in 1860. It was a huge honor that Martin took quite seriously, but he was already one of the most successful entrepreneurs in the city with plenty on his plate.

Born during the year 1819 in the small town of Paris, New York, Martin had received a typical education in school while working in his family's flour mill. Sadly, his father passed away when he was just fourteen. As the newly appointed man of the house, he decided to take the $900 he had saved and travel to Chicago in hopes of finding something to invest in. He came across a few offers there, but nothing really caught his eye. He decided to save his money and return home. At twenty-three, he moved to Michigan and worked his way up to the head of several different companies in Ann Arbor, Dexter and Delhi. It was in Delhi that he built his own flour mill.

In 1844, Martin married a woman named Submit Desdemona Higgins. She was the daughter of a New York lumber baron and known for her great beauty. By all accounts, she was intelligent and strong-willed. Her biggest pet peeve was her first name, Submit. She considered it a blight on her birth certificate and refused to answer to it. She went by her middle name, Desdemona.

Together, the couple moved to Grand Rapids in 1846 and started their family, which would come to include a daughter named Mattie and two sons, Cassius and Frank. Over the following years, Martin would find himself embarking on many different ventures—everything from mills to furniture and cattle—and he excelled at every one of them. Martin brought the first Holstein-Friesian cattle to Michigan; his farm stood where the Kent Country Club currently resides on Sweet Street and College Avenue NE. He built the first grain elevator in town close to the railroad, making it easy for him to sell and ship the grain by rail.

Martin also bought the first real bank in Grand Rapids and named it the M.L. Sweet & Company Exchange Bank. It eventually merged with the First National Bank and became Old National Bank. (After Martin's death, Old National merged with Kent Mutual to become Old Kent Bank, which was subsequently acquired by Fifth Third Bancorp in 1994.)

When Martin was persuaded to run for mayor on the Republican ticket, he wasn't sure how it would turn out, since the town was predominantly Democratic. However, everyone admired Martin's work ethic and his generous spirit. He was known for always extending a helping hand to others, and that carried a lot of weight with the public. He ended up winning by a landslide.

At the time, Fulton Street was known as home to only the most prominent members of society—a street for the elite. Martin wanted to be part of it. He and Desdemona purchased two lots on the southwest corner of Fulton Street and Lafayette Avenue from Martin Ryerson and hired Rueben Wheeler as architect. The magnificent home was completed around 1863 and remains there to this day.

The Sweet family loved their new house and continued to be active in the community. They were steadfast members of First (Park) Congregational Church and donated a large sum of money to help fund the new church, eventually built on East Park Place and Library Street—just blocks away from their home.

In the entryways of upper-class homes, it was common to keep a basket in which visitors could drop their calling cards. Looking like today's business cards, they were a way for people to advertise who was in their extended circle, like "friending" on social media. People would leave their card to express appreciation for a dinner party, offer condolences or let the homeowner know they stopped by when no one was home. In the Sweets' entryway, Desdemona had a marble table with a basket on it for these cards and insisted an eight-foot pier glass mirror be attached to the back of it so she could look herself over before leaving the home. On Sundays, townsfolk could be seen lining up on Fulton Street as if a parade was coming. They were there to get a glimpse of what Desdemona was wearing to church.

The former home of the Sweet family. *Brad Donaldson.*

Desdemona loved the sensation she caused when she gracefully descended the front steps and walked to the street where her carriage waited for her. The crowds were never disappointed. She was well known for her fashion sense, always wearing the latest designs. Velvet wraps and silk brocades were not commonly worn in Grand Rapids at that time, so she was a sight to see.

When it came time to run for a second term as mayor, Martin declined to put his name in the hat again. He also rejected his "generous" salary of one dollar—which the City of Grand Rapids still owes him.

Martin had a duplex home built on the lot directly south at 17–19 Lafayette for his two married sons and their wives. There was even an underground tunnel built between the two homes. It's been said that the brothers' wives didn't get along very well, so they didn't live there long. One can't help but wonder if it may have had more to do with the fact that their in-laws could show up at any moment through the connected passageway. No matter the reason, it was rented out soon after they moved, and the tunnel was filled in. In the basement of the duplex, you can still see where the entrance to the tunnel was. The duplex is now known as the Chateau Lafayette.

In 1868, Martin sold out of the milling business and built the Sweet's Hotel on the corner of Canal and Pearl Streets by the east channel of the Grand River. Today, most people know the corner as the old part of the

The former duplex of Martin and Desdemona's two sons. *Brad Donaldson.*

Sweet's Hotel on Monroe Avenue. *Courtesy of the Grand Rapids Public Museum Collection.*

Amway Hotel. Martin spared no expense; the hotel opened in 1869 at a cost of $150,000. But the location of the hotel had issues. The corner on which it sat had a sharp turn and a steep, four-foot grade difference between Canal Street and Monroe Avenue. This sharp curve was a nightmare for horse-drawn wagons to navigate, and the lower ground had problems with flooding every spring. As a solution, in 1870, the Common Council voted to raise Canal Street four feet. Martin's was the largest structure that had to be raised. By all accounts, it was quite the sight. In all, 1,800 screw jacks were put under the building, and at the signal of a whistle, workers would give a turn all at the same time to raise the building up evenly, a quarter of an inch with each turn.

The early years were good ones for the Sweet family, but life seemed to get harder in the latter half of their lives. In December 1890, their son Frank became seriously ill with typhoid fever. He wasn't expected to make a full recovery but, with time, managed to do so. Unfortunately, on December 6 the same year, Desdemona died in their home of pneumonia at ten o'clock in the morning after three days of suffering. She was seventy-two years old. Knowing how she felt about her name, Martin had her tombstone engraved, "Desdemona S. Higgins—Wife of Martin L. Sweet." Even in death, Desdemona's reputation continued to be one of high standing.

One year later, Martin married a woman named Emma Pegg McBrian, who had been Desdemona's companion in the last years of her life. She was twenty-seven years younger than Martin, and he was quite proud of the fact that she agreed to the matrimony. Emma was described as a raven-haired, buxom lady who, although forty-five, looked ten years younger. According to the *Allegan Gazette* on July 25, 1891, when Martin was handed the marriage license, he "seemed as pleased with it as a boy contemplating his first safety bicycle."

They had less than two good years together before the economic depression hit and caused the Panic of 1893. Martin was highly leveraged, and his financial empire came crashing down. A judge foreclosed on his loans, and Martin found himself owing creditors over $150,000. This resulted in his properties being sold. In 1898, Sweet's Hotel and his 128 acres of land with livestock, as well as other properties in Grand Rapids, Newaygo and Mason County, were auctioned off to the highest bidder. The only thing he managed to keep was his family home on Fulton Street.

Despite having once reigned over the city of Grand Rapids, Martin wasn't too proud to take an available job at the local garbage dump, burning trash for a small daily wage. While Martin was worth over half a million dollars at one point, he was close to penniless when he died. He passed away at home from the flu on February 21, 1905. It was his eighty-sixth birthday. Emma continued to live in the house for several years until she moved to Ontario to stay with her daughter. She only occasionally visited Grand Rapids to look after the property. She died on March 16, 1914, after being ill for several months.

The home was then leased to Frank M. Davis. His wife, Clara, was a piano teacher and a founding member of St. Cecilia's Music Society. (In fact, the script lettering of the words "St. Cecilia" on the face of the cornerstone is said to be etched in Clara's handwriting and was used for years as the society's logo.) It was through her efforts that the world-renowned concert pianist Ottokar Malek established a music school in the house from 1914 to 1919. Teachers came in from Chicago and took the bedrooms, so the Malek family moved their personal belongings up into the attic and used that for their private quarters. Once the school closed, the home was used as a boardinghouse until 1927, when it was purchased by the Women's City Club.

Founded in 1924, the Women's City Club is a private social group that brings together women of all ages, backgrounds and interests. To this day, the club continues to offer educational classes, enrichment programs and many other opportunities to become involved in the community. The women took their job as stewards of the Sweet House quite seriously. Extensive renovations were made, adding an auditorium, a large dining area that they fittingly named Desdemona's Dining Room and a smaller dining room named the Wedgwood Room. They also collected an incredible number of antiques throughout the home, like the bronze clock that was purchased by the Sweet family in 1860 and a rosette table desk that dates to the Civil War.

Anyone who owns a home understands how expensive upkeep can be. The price is only multiplied when trying to maintain a Heritage Hill mansion that's over 160 years old. To raise funds for the maintenance of this landmark, the Sweet House Foundation was formed in 2005 and incorporated the following year. In 2018, the Women's City Club moved out of the Sweet House. The Sweet House Foundation assumed full responsibility for the care of the historic home. It is now a popular event venue for weddings, parties, dining, meetings and more.

The Haunting

I was invited to have my first tour of Martin's home in 2015 by the historical consultant of the Sweet House Foundation, Carol Dodge. I felt a little out of my league walking up to the home and knocking on the door. As soon as it opened, I was struck by Carol's beautiful blue eyes and warm smile. She gave me the friendliest greeting, and I instantly felt like I was with a friend. Being a former Women's City Club president, Carol's respect for the home was apparent. In fact, she has written a book titled *The Mayor, the Musician, and the Mansion: Martin Sweet, Ottokar Malek, and the Sweet House*, so be sure to check it out!

Carol told me that the house had been rumored to be haunted for a long time. While doing research, she had found a story that took place in 1936 after a Thursday performance. Some Victorian chairs were brought to the auditorium and set up on stage for the upcoming recital. The program drew in a large crowd and was followed by a luncheon that went on longer than expected. By the end, the manager was exhausted and told the custodian they would put things back in place the following day. The next morning, they found all the chairs on the stage knocked over, despite no one being in the house. It seems Desdemona was not pleased that her home was left in disarray.

Strangely, fifty-five years later, the exact same thing happened. A party lasted late into the evening, so the manager and the custodian decided to wait until the following day to pick up. They were speechless when they walked in. They were the last to leave on Thursday and the first to arrive on Friday morning, yet all the chairs were flipped over. At this point, they had security alarms on the building, and none had gone off—proving no one had entered or exited the structure.

Portraits of Martin and Desdemona were found in the attic when it was being cleaned out. Realizing the treasure they had, the ladies instantly hung them in the hallway. They went out of their way to order name plaques for the frames, but whoever ordered them did not know that Desdemona's deep disdain for her first name had carried over into the afterlife. When they hung up the plaque reading, "Submit Desdemona Sweet," it stayed on for a day or two but was soon found on the floor. Thinking it must not have adhered well, they made sure it was solidly attached. The next morning, however, they found it on the floor again. Jokes began to fly that Desdemona was not happy and was pulling it off every night. At that point, the women busted out the superglue and, once and for all, made sure the plaque was going to stay. That's when activity ramped up.

The sound of youngsters running through the home could be heard, particularly in the attic. Martin was known to keep toy trains up there for his children and grandchildren to play with. While growing up, Mattie, Frank and Cassius also loved to climb up to the peak of their home, known as a belvedere, a windowed gallery that gives a panoramic view of the city. Desdemona was also known to use these windows to see when Martin was on his way home from work.

Mary Jane Riegling was the Women's City Club office manager for over twenty years and was quite vocal about her experiences. She would sit in a small office on the first floor that looked out into the main hallway at the back of the building. One day when she was there alone, she watched a man dressed in old-fashioned clothing walk by her doorway and disappear down the hall. He didn't say a word or even acknowledge her existence. When she got up to look for him, he was gone.

Other times, Mary Jane would hear a piano in the Best Room play on its own. The first time it happened, it scared her to death. She grabbed a letter opener and crept around the corner. The music would always stop when she entered the room. This happened to her so many times, she got used to it.

Another member told me that when she was treasurer, she would come in before everyone else to take care of paperwork. After using her key to enter the home, she deliberately locked the door behind her for her own safety. She joked that she was an older lady and wouldn't be "much of a match against an intruder." One day, she went upstairs to start working and had only been sitting at her desk for a couple minutes when she heard piano music.

I was the only one in the house at the time and assumed a radio must have somehow turned on. Then I realized it was the piano in the Best Room. I went down the steps with my knees shaking and slowly walked into the room. As I did, I saw the piano keys moving on their own—until they stopped dead. I was terrified! I was told that when Desdemona and her son were sick, they had moved both of their beds into the Best Room so the nurse could tend to them easier. They said Desdemona died in there. Maybe it was her? We also know it's the room where they laid bodies out for viewing when they died.

After she witnessed that, she always made sure another living person was in the house with her.

A chef named Laurel, who worked for the kitchen from 2002 through 2009, also felt the spirits around her. One morning, she had come in to do some prep work for an afternoon event. She kept hearing a faint whistling. Standing at the kitchen counter cleaning vegetables, she was overcome with the feeling that she wasn't alone. Seconds later, a huge gust of wind blew behind her, strong enough to rattle the pots and pans. Still standing at the counter, she looked to the left and caught a glimpse of someone walking directly behind her, moving quickly in the opposite direction. Quickly turning her head to the right, she caught a glimpse of a long green dress dragging on the floor around the corner. She told everyone, "I know it was Desdemona."

These are just a handful of the many stories I gathered during my first visit. In 2020, I began to work on this book and was hoping to get permission to do a paranormal investigation with my team. I contacted Sue Pemberton, the general manager at the time. Sue was not aware of the ghostly activity when she first took the position, but she had grown up in a haunted house and quickly tuned in to what was going on at her new place of employment.

Sue was in the kitchen one day when she found that the heavy door to the walk-in cooler had opened on its own. Another time, cups and a coffee pot flew off the kitchen counter and landed several feet away on the floor. What was impressive was despite the pot being full, nothing had spilled, and the pot was left spinning in circles. Another time, late at night, she was standing in the kitchen looking out through the little window into the dining room and saw the back of a man's head. He stood about five feet, seven inches, but there were no men in the home that night.

Sue ran my request to study the Sweet House by the Sweet House Foundation board of directors. Imagine my delight when I was granted access for one night. Due to COVID-19 and snowy weather, the investigation didn't happen until March 6, 2021. Most investigations are performed with the intention of determining if a location is haunted, but that was not the case for the Sweet House. Many reputable people have had experiences in this home for years. My goal was to gather evidence to support those claims.

The night began with Carol Dodge giving the rest of my team the tour. Tamara Steil, the Sweet House Foundation president at the time, was kind enough to stop by and introduce herself. After welcoming us, everyone but our team and the assistant manager left. We started by shutting our cell phones off and putting them away—as they can create false readings on several pieces of the equipment we use. We did a base reading throughout the entire building, including the attic. Depending on the room, the temperature held steady between fifty-nine and sixty-seven degrees. While chilly, it was not drafty. There were no unusual readings on the gauss meter or electromagnetic field detector. We set up our equipment and got to work.

Desdemona's
spectral mirror
ghost. *Roger Scholz.*

Countless people had shared stories about the security system going off on its own. The manager was consistently called in the middle of the night by the police, letting her know the alarm was sounding and there was a suspected break-in. She would rush to the home to see that everything was fine, except for an inside door or two being ajar. Knowing this, we tried to see what doors would naturally open on their own; none of them did. They were heavy doors, unmovable without a strong breeze or other force. We had noted that the door to the butler's pantry in the Wedgwood Room was open at a ninety-degree angle. The Wedgwood Room holds a fourteen-foot-by-five-foot mahogany table that is quite striking—even more so when you learn that four men who became United States presidents have dined at it (Taft, McKinley, Ford and Theodore Roosevelt). Two hours into our investigation,

The Sweet spirits. *Roger Scholz.*

the door to the butler's pantry closed on its own. Excitedly, we went to review our video camera that had been aimed at the door, only to find that the newly charged battery was completely dead and the camera was off.

Whatever was in the home with us seemed to favor two pieces of equipment we were using on our hunt. The first was our Kinect SLS Camera. If you have never seen this camera, it shoots out a pattern of infrared lights, and anything that is three-dimensional (like a person) will appear on the screen as a stick figure. It uses an infrared light projector that shows everything as dots arranged in 3D formations. These infrared dots allow the camera to show depth and detail. Then the camera employs a software program that recognizes joints and movement and creates stick figures. The second piece of equipment was a spirit box, a device that utilizes radio frequencies by sweeping stations to generate white noise. The belief is that it can provide an entity the energy it needs to be heard. While the sound could be voices coming through the static from radio stations, it is quite compelling when the voices seem to answer your questions or give intellectual responses—particularly in multiple words or sentences.

We hunkered down in the Best Room with the SLS camera pointing toward the fireplace, with armchairs on both sides of the frame. Jeff Sytsma, my historian friend, sat in the chair on the right. My team members Brad Donaldson, Bob Webster and Roger Scholz were also in the room, sitting down. We started the spirit box and began recording.

"Desdemona, are you here with us tonight?" Roger asked. "I just want to let you know you have a beautiful home." Almost immediately, a figure appeared on the SLS camera, sitting in the chair to the left of the fireplace, the only empty chair in the room.

I got excited and said, "We've got company! Sitting in the chair right there…Well, hello!" At that point, we all heard an unexplained knocking noise followed by a female voice saying, "Hi" from the spirit box.

"Welcome to the room!" said Roger.

We all heard the same female voice say, "Thank you, thank you." The figure stayed in the chair for about two minutes before disappearing.

After a couple uneventful minutes, I said, "If anybody is here with us, if you stand over by the fireplace, we'll be able to pick your picture up on this camera." As if in response, we heard, "Okay" on the spirit box.

Jeff asked, "Did you build a tunnel, or was it someone else's idea?"

"I did," came a man's voice from the spirit box.

Again, hoping for more visual proof, I urged: "Can you take a seat by the fireplace again?" Instantly, a figure reappeared on the SLS camera, sitting in the chair waving to us.

We ended the session soon after and went to get our additional video camera off the mantel. The camera, which had been fully charged only minutes before, had zero battery left. On recharging it, we found it had only recorded one minute and fifty-six seconds of video before shutting itself off. The shutdown occurred at the exact same time we captured the first figure on the SLS camera. (We have since used this camera in other investigations and have had no further malfunctions.)

We then went upstairs into the Victorian Room, where Desdemona's mirror now sits. We set up several cameras, including one angled at the mirror, and began recording at 8:09 p.m. I was across the room, looking into the SLS camera, when I saw what appeared to be a figure coming out of the mirror and lingering above Brad, who was sitting in a chair. The figure floated around for a couple minutes and then disappeared. Jeff saw something in the screen of the camcorder at the exact same time I thought I saw a figure in the hallway. Roger heard us gasp and said, "What did you see, Jules?" The spirit box then spoke up again: "Watch me." Suddenly, a very large figure showed up on the SLS camera, coming straight out of the mirror. It danced in the air for a couple minutes before going back into the mirror. Some paranormal experts believe mirrors are portals to the other side. Seeing how easily these figures came and went through the glass led me to believe there may be some truth in that.

Later in the night, we were upstairs in the Yellow Room, which was Martin and Desdemona's master bedroom, when we caught three messages on the spirit box. Within two minutes, we captured a female voice saying, "Go downstairs," "Wet" and "Treat it." When we went into the basement later that night, we came across a flood in one of the locked rooms. The assistant manager had to call a service in to get it taken care of. It seems Desdemona continues to keep an eye on things.

My team had a myriad of experiences during our time in the Sweet House, but to me, it was all summed up during our last spirit box session. With all of us present, it captured the following words: "I'm here. For better…or worse. Legacy. Family. Desdemona."

BIBLIOGRAPHY

Ancestry. https://www.ancestry.com/.

Baxter, Albert. *History of the City of Grand Rapids, Michigan*. Munsell, 1891.

GenealogyBank.com.

Grand Rapids Herald (various articles).

Grand Rapids Press (various articles).

HistoryGrandRapids.org. http://historygrandrapids.org.

Michigan Tradesman. "Gone Beyond: Death of the Oldest Merchant in Grand Rapids." October 1906.

R.L. Polk. Grand Rapids City Directories.

About the Author

J ulie Rathsack works as a manager of business insights during the day but switches to history buff and ghost fanatic at night. She cowrote the best-selling book *Ghosts of Grand Rapids* and began doing ghost tours in 2015. She is the vice president and research director for the West Michigan Ghost Hunters Society (founded in 1999) and has investigated countless locations in and outside of Michigan. With all her work on local history and experience with Grand Rapids' paranormal, Julie is considered the expert on ghosts in her city. A graduate of Grand Rapids Community College (GRCC), Julie earned an associate degree in liberal arts. She resides in Grand Rapids with her husband, Dave, and their two sons, David and Samuel.

FREE eBOOK OFFER

Scan the QR code below, enter your e-mail address and get our original Haunted America compilation eBook delivered straight to your inbox for free.

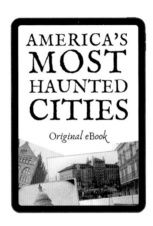

ABOUT THE BOOK

Every city, town, parish, community and school has their own paranormal history. Whether they are spirits caught in the Bardo, ancestors checking on their descendants, restless souls sending a message or simply spectral troublemakers, ghosts have been part of the human tradition from the beginning of time.

In this book, we feature a collection of stories from five of America's most haunted cities: Baltimore, Chicago, Galveston, New Orleans and Washington, D.C.

SCAN TO GET
AMERICA'S MOST HAUNTED CITIES

Having trouble scanning? Go to:
biz.arcadiapublishing.com/americas-most-haunted-cities